Grammar

For class or self-study

Ana Acavedo
Carol Lethaby
Jeremy Harmer
with Cheryl Pelteret

Marshall Cavendish
Education

© 2007 Marshall Cavendish Education

First published 2007 by Marshall Cavendish Education
Marshall Cavendish is a member of the Times Publishing Group

ISBN: (10-digit) 0 462 00775 8
      (13-digit) 978 04620 0775 5

Marshall Cavendish Education
119 Wardour Street
London W1F 0UW

Designed by Hart McLeod, Cambridge
Illustrations by Jo Taylor, Yane Christiansen, Francis Fung, Rory Walker,
Valeryia Steadman, Tim Oliver

Printed and bound by Times Offset (M) Sdn Bhd

Contents

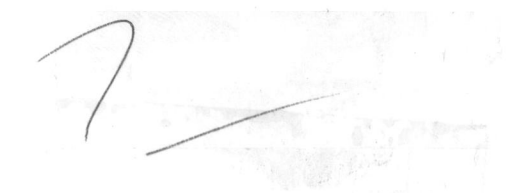

Introduction

To the student

Welcome to Just Grammar. You can use this book with other students and a teacher, or you can work alone with it.

In this book you will find clear explanations of the grammar you need at this level. There are examples to help you understand the explanations too. Each unit has exercises for you to practise your grammar.

When you see this symbol (☞) it means that the answers to the practice exercises are in the answer key at the back of the book. You can check your answers there.

You can look at the contents page to find the grammar you want to understand and practise.

We are sure that this book will help you to progress in English.

To the teacher

This book is part of a series designed to be used alone or to supplement any course book you may be using. Each book in the series specialises in either language skills or (as in the case of *Just Grammar*) in aspects of the English language. It can be used either in class or by students working on their own.

Just Grammar consists of 32 units which offer comprehensive grammar explanations, and provide practice activities to ensure the student's ability to use the language. Apart from the last two review units, the organisation is alphabetical. Users should look in the contents list on page 3 to see which area of grammar they wish to work on.

Students will be able to use *Just Grammar* without needing explanation or guidance on the part of the teacher. Having read through the explanations and examples in the book, they can do the exercises, and then check them in the comprehensive answer key at the back. However, the units are also highly appropriate for work in class.

We are confident that you will find this book a real asset and we recommend that you also try the other books in the series: *Just Reading and Writing, Just Vocabulary* and *Just Listening and Speaking.*

Comparative adjectives & adverbs

Use comparative adjectives (and adverbs) with **than**.
> He's older **than** my brother.
> The red ones are more expensive **than** the blue ones.
> He ran faster **than** me.

For short adjectives and adverbs: add **-er**.
> tall – taller
> fast – faster

For short adjectives with vowel + consonant: final letter x 2 + **-er**.
> hot – hotter
> thin – thinner

For short adjectives which end in -y: y̶ = i + er.
> noisy – noisier
> ugly – uglier

For adverbs that end with -ly: **more** + adverb.
> She eats **more** quickly than I do.
> Dogs eat **more** noisily than cats.

For long adjectives: **more** + adjective.
> beautiful – **more** beautiful
> comfortable – **more** comfortable

Some common adjectives (and adverbs) have their own special forms.
> good (well) – **better**
> bad (badly) – **worse**

. . . .

1 Complete the table. Put the words in the correct columns.

one syllable e.g. big	two syllables e.g. heavy	three syllables e.g. unhappy

beautiful fast high large popular tall small sunny friendly

Can you add more adjectives to the columns?

2 Read the country facts in the table and complete the sentences.
Use the comparative form of any suitable adjectives from the box.

| big   great   few   high   large |
| low   many   small   tall |

	South Africa	Canada	UK
Population	42,718,530	32,507,874	60,270,708
Official languages	11	2	1
Internet users	3.1 million	16.11 million	25 million
Size	1,219,912 sq km	9,984,670 sq km	244,820 sq km
Highest point	Njesuthi 3,408 m	Mount Logan 5,959 m	Ben Nevis 1,343 m
Coastline	2,798 km	202,080 km	12,429 km

There are (a) ...more... people living in the UK than in Canada.

Of the three countries mentioned, Canada has a (b) smaller .... population than South Africa and the UK.

South Africa has (c) ...many..... official languages than the UK, which has only one – English. The UK has (d) ...low......... official languages than Canada, which has two, English and French.

A (e) .... number of people use the Internet in Canada than in South Africa.

South Africa is much (f) .... than the UK, but it is (g) .... than Canada.

Njesuthi is (h) .... than Mount Logan, but it is much (i) .... than Ben Nevis.

Canada's coastline is (j) .... than Britain's coastline.

- -

3 Complete the sentences with the comparative form of the adjectives and adverbs in brackets.
Add 'than' only where necessary.

a Cities are ...more interesting than...... (interesting) .... beaches, but you can relax
   .... (easily) at the beach.

b The food in Australia was .... (good) here, and you could eat
   .... (cheaply), too!

c Where is the public transport .... (fast), in London or in Dublin? In Dublin,
   probably, and Dublin is .... (small), so you can walk.

d I find travelling by train .... (comfortable) travelling by car and you can also get to
   your destination .... (quickly).

e In July, plane fares to New Zealand are .... (low) in December. But it's
   .... (cold) then, because it's winter there.

4 Look at the pictures on page 9. Use the prompts to write sentences. The first one is done for you.

a Stadium Australia / the Millennium stadium _Stadium Australia is larger than the Millennium Stadium._

b Edmonton Stadium / Stadium Australia _Edmonton Stadium is smaller than the Stadium Australia_

c Kingda Ka / Top Thrill Dragster _Kingda Ka is taller than Top Thrill Dragster_

d In Australia, horse racing / rugby league _In Australia is horse racing more popular than ragby league_

e Pipeline bungee / Mokai Canyon bungee _Pipeline bungee is higher than Mokai Canyon bungee_

f In Britain, football / cricket _In Britian is football more popular than cricket_

g The Millennium Stadium / Edmonton Stadium _The Millennium Stadium is more bigger than Edmonton Stadium_

h In the USA, American football / basketball _In the USA basketball more popular than American football_

5 Now answer the questions about the places in the pictures.

a Which rollercoaster is taller – The Big One, or Kingda Ka? _Kingda Ka is taller than The Big One._

b Is rugby more or less popular on TV in Britain, than cricket? _Rugby is more popular on TV in Britain than cricket_

c Which sport is less popular on TV in the USA, baseball or basketball? _In the USA is baseball more less than basketball_

d Is the Edmonton Stadium in Canada smaller or bigger than Australia Stadium? _Edmonton Stadium is smaller than Australia Stadium_

e Which bungee jump is higher – the one in New Zealand or South Africa? _South Africa bungee is higher than in New zeland_

f In which country is horse racing less popular on TV than football? _In Australia horse racing less popular then football on TV_

Large stadiums

Millennium Stadium, Cardiff, Wales	72,500 seats
Stadium Australia, Sydney, Australia	110,000 seats
Edmonton Stadium, Canada	60,000 seats

Mokai Canyon, New Zealand	80 m
Plettenberg Bay, South Africa	216 m
Pipeline Bungee, Australia	102 m

High bungee jumps

Tall roller coasters

Kingda Ka, New Jersey, USA	456 feet
Top Thrill Dragster, Cedar Point, Ohio, USA	420 feet
The Big One, Blackpool, England	235 feet

Australia: 1. Australian Rules football
2. Horse racing 3. Rugby League

Britain: 1. Football / soccer 2. Rugby 3. Cricket

USA: 1. Baseball 2. American football
3. Basketball

Popular sports on television

Superlative adjectives

He's	the	oldest man	in the world.
It's		most beautiful film	I've ever seen.

He	sang	the	fastest.
She	drove		most carefully.

Use superlative adjectives and adverbs with **the.**
> He's **the oldest** person in the world.
> They're **the most beautiful** paintings I've ever seen.
> He climbed **the most carefully.**

For short adjectives: add **-est.**
> tall – tall**est**
> fast – fast**est**

For short adjectives with vowel + consonant: final letter x 2 + **-est.**
> hot – hot**test**
> thin – thi**nnest**

Short adjectives which end in -y: y̶ = i + **est.**
> noisy – nois**iest**
> ugly – ugl**iest**

For adverbs that end with -ly: **most** + adverb.
> She eats the **most** quickly.
> Dogs eat the **most** noisily.

For long adjectives: **most** + adjective.
> beautiful – **most** beautiful
> comfortable – **most** comfortable

Some common adjectives (and adverbs) have their own special forms.
> good (well) – **best**
> bad (badly) – **worst**

- -

1 Make the following into superlative adjectives.

a bad ....

b boring ....

c cheap ....

d cramped ....

e deep ....

f expensive ....

g fast ....

h fat ....

i funny ....

j good ....

k high ....

l interesting ....

m long ....

n narrow ....

o spacious ....

p thin ....

q ugly ....

r uncomfortable ....

2 Complete these sentences using the superlative form of the adjective in brackets.

a This is ...... *the worst* .... (bad) film I have ever seen!

b *A Brief History of Time* is .... (interesting) book I have ever read.

c Would you like to live in .... (large) city in the world?

d I think this is .... (uncomfortable) chair I have ever sat in.

e They went to .... (cheap) restaurant in the city, because they had very little money.

f The Lamborghini Mucielago is one of .... (expensive) cars in the world.

g Charlie Chaplin's films are still some of .... (funny) movies ever.

h What do you think is .... (good) way to get to the bridge from here?

i Try to cross the river here, because this is .... (narrow) part.

j Richie is .... (thin) of my three nephews.

3 Read the advertisements. Answer the questions, using the superlative forms of the adjectives.

A
2-bedroomed flat in quiet street 40 minutes from town centre. Not near transport. Large windows - very light. Modern kitchen and bathroom. Garden - good for children. £200 per week.

B
Small, cosy 1-bedroomed flat. Bathroom and kitchen need some work - a bit old-fashioned. Small windows - not very sunny. In busy town centre - transport no problem. £100 per week.

C
3-bedroomed flat in countryside. One hour by train to city centre. Large windows and glass roof in kitchen! Fairly modern. £150 per week.

Which flat is the ...?

a (small) ...... *Flat B is the smallest.* ....

b (sunny) ....

c (large) ....

d (near) to town ....

e (modern) ....

f (noisy) ....

g (expensive) ....

4 Now write sentences using the opposites of the superlative adjectives you have written in exercise 3.

Flat C is the largest. ....

....

....

....

....

5 Read 'The Top Three' in the table, and make sentences. The first one has been done for you.

The Top Three	1	2	3
Long rivers	Nile	Amazon	Yangtze-Kiang
Tall telecommunications towers	CN Tower, Canada	Ostankino Tower, Russia	Oriental Pearl Broadcasting Tower, China
Large countries	Russia	Canada	China
High waterfalls	Angel, Venezuela	Tugela, South Africa	Utigård, Norway
Deep caves	Lamprechtshofen, Austria	Gouffre Mirolda, France	Reseau Jean Bernard, France
Crowded cities	Hong Kong, China	Lagos, Nigeria	Dhaka, Bangladesh

a   *The longest river is the Nile.* ....

b   ....

c   ....

d   ....

e   ....

f   ....

6 Look at the photos on page 13 and complete these sentences. Use the superlative form of the adjectives in the box.

long
expensive
old
small
far

The (a) .... female twins were Kin Narita and Gin Kanie (born 1892, Japan), whose names mean *gold* and *silver*. Gin lived the (b) .... : she died in 2001, aged 108, and her sister Kin died the year before, aged 107.

The (c) .... orange nose push was achieved by Myles Anderson, who pushed an orange with his nose for 1.6 km, in London. This took 1 hour and 14 minutes.

The (d) .... production car was the Peel P50, which was 134 cm long, 99 cm wide and 134 cm high. It was made in Britain in the 1960s.

The (e) .... guitar was sold for $957,500, in 2002. It had belonged to Jerry Garcia, of the band *The Grateful Dead*.

UNIT 3

-ing & *-ed* adjectives

Use **-ed** adjectives to say how you feel.
I am interest**ed**.
I am bor**ed**.
Use **-ing** adjectives to talk about something or somebody else.
He is bor**ing**.
This book is excit**ing**.

1   **Circle the correct words in the dialogues.**

> GIRL 1:   Let's do something. I'm so (**a**) *boring / bored*.
>
> GIRL 2:   Yes. It's (**b**) *boring / bored* here. Let's go out.

> MAN: I'm going to watch this DVD about Jamaica. Are you (**c**) *interesting / interested*?
>
> WOMAN: Yes, It sounds (**d**) *interesting / interested*.

> MAN: You can't come with us? How (**e**) *disappointing / disappointed*.
>
> WOMAN: I'm (**f**) *disappointing / disappointed* too. Next time, maybe.

2   **Choose the correct adjective for each blank. Does it end in *-ed* or *-ing*?**

a I find swimming very ....*relaxing*........... (relax).

b Learning about other cultures is very .... (interest).

c I am .... (interest) in travelling.

d Jude was very .... (tire) after the long trip.

e Sharon thinks flying is .... (tire).

f The plane moved up and down but all the people were completely .... (relax).

g I was .... (worry) about the long flight.

h James finds my accent .... (amuse).

i The film was very .... (amuse). I laughed a lot.

3 Read the postcards. Write the letter of the correct picture in the boxes.

1 Here I am in England, finally! I'm so
(a) <u>excited</u> / exciting! Some things are
(b) surprised / surprising, some are even
(c) shocked / shocking. The weather is particularly (d) interested / interesting. Today it rained all day and it was cold. Now, at 9 p.m., the sun is shining! One thing is sure: things are different but never
(e) bored / boring!
Wish you were here! David

a

Have a cuppa

Picture ☐

2 'How about a cuppa?' That's what my friend asks me all the time! She means 'a cup of tea'. Here people drink tea when they are cold, or hot, when they are (f) tired / tiring, or (g) relaxed / relaxing ... tea always makes you feel better! But nobody has the famous four o'clock tea, like it says in our English book. That's very
(h) disappointed / disappointing!
Lucy

b

English weather

Picture ☐

4 Underline the correct word in the postcards. The first one is done for you.

5 Complete each sentence with the correct *-ing* or *-ed* adjective made from the verb in brackets.

a Driving on the left was a bit ....*frightening*.... (frighten) at first.

b I am a bit .... (worry) about my English.

c I went to a cricket match. It was long and .... (bore).

d English food is very good. That's .... (surprise), isn't it?

e People say English humour is very .... (amuse), but I don't understand it.

f I am .... (interest) in British pop music.

Articles

a, an

Use **a** to talk about one of something.

> **a** car   **a** song

Use **an** to talk about one of something before a vowel (or something like a vowel).

> **an** eye   **an** hour

the

Use **the** to talk about something special that we all know about.

> **the** world   **the** future

Use **the** to talk about something for the second time, or when people know which one it is.

> It's a painting by Leonardo da Vinci. **The** painting is in Paris.
>
> Pass me **the** cup in front of you.

Use **the** to talk about the names of some countries with more than one word or which end with 'of something'.

> **The** People's Republic of China   **The** United States of America

Zero article (= no article)

Don't use **a, an** or **the** for plural nouns which describe things <u>in general</u>.

> I love _ flowers.
>
> People often complain about _ noise.

Don't use **a, an** or **the** for uncountable nouns (see above) about things <u>in general</u>.

> I like _ milk.
>
> I don't eat _ meat.

Don't use **a, an** or **the** with the names of most countries.

> He went to _ Russia.
>
> I've never been to _ Pakistan.

---

1   Say why no article is used in each one of the examples 1 – 6.

a zero article before a plural noun describing things in general	1 I've never eaten snails. ....*a*........
	2 She lived in France for ten years. ....
b zero article before uncountable nouns describing things in general	3 Do you like rice? ....
	4 When did she move to Kenya? ....
c zero article before most names of countries	5 No, I don't like cats. ....
	6 I never drink coffee in the evening. ....

2 Complete these paragraphs with **a**, **an**, **the**, or zero article.

(a) ....*The*.... Eiffel Tower in Paris was built between 1887 and 1889. (b) .... architect was Stephen Sauvestre. There is (c) .... restaurant on the second level called (d) .... Jules Verne restaurant and there is (e) .... restaurant on the first level called Altitude 95. There are (f) .... shops on the third level and of course there is (g) .... great view of (h) .... city. There are 1,665 steps to (i) .... top of (j) .... tower, but there is also (k) .... elevator.

3 Match the explanations (a – h) with examples (1 – 8) from the text about Zaha Hadid.

Zaha Hadid is an architect. But she's not your usual architect! For a start, she's a woman. *She grew up in Iraq. She wears bright, shiny jewellery*, and has been described as "a big woman, with *an even more gigantic personality*". She has quite a stormy nature, but as her friends put it, 'she's actually very *good with people*, and *the storms are all on the outside*'. She designed an award-winning opera house for the city of Cardiff, but when the public decided they didn't want an opera house, but a football stadium instead, *the opera house* was never built.

The Cincinnati Museum of Contemporary Art in *the USA*, is one of her designs.

a We use **a** to talk about one of something.

b We use **an** if the next word starts with a vowel sound.

c We use **the** with some country names with more than one word or which end with '… of something' (e.g. The People's Republic of China).

d We use **the** when we mention something for the second time.

e We use **the** when we talk about a special thing (or things) that we all know about.

f We don't use **a**, **an** or **the** for the names of most countries (or cities).

g We don't use **a**, **an** or **the** with plural nouns which describe things in general.

h We don't use **a**, **an** or **the** when we talk about uncountable nouns.

1 an even more gigantic personality ....

2 she grew up in Iraq ....

3 she wears bright shiny jewellery ....

4 she's a woman ....

5 she's good with people ....

6 the opera house ....

7 the storms are on the outside ....

8 the USA ....

4 Put **a**, **an**, **the** or nothing in the gaps in the following sentences.

a Magda comes from .... Poland. She lives in .... Warsaw.

b She's .... actress and does most of her work on .... national radio station.

c Her house is full of .... modern furniture, except for .... furniture in her dining room. That's very 'brown' and old.

d .... Polish people love Magda, and now she is working for .... international radio station.

e .... fan (a member of the public who likes her) wrote her .... letter. .... letter was very long, but Magda likes .... letters like that.

f Last summer she went on holiday in .... West Indies.

g She visited .... different islands, but didn't have time to see them all.

h Next month, Magda is going to .... United States. She wants to work in .... films there.

i '.. film industry is very important in .... America,' she says. 'I have .... dreams, but .... big dream of my life is to be a Hollywood actress!'

5 Read sentences a – i and match the use of the article a, an or the with reasons 1 – 6 for using it.

a I want to buy a new car. ......**1**......

b My brother is an artist. ....

c Don't stay in the sun too long! ....

d Which kitten do you want? The black one or the grey one? ....

e Have you been to the United Kingdom? ....

f The first man walked on the moon in 1969. ....

g I need a hammer. Can you pass me the hammer, please. ....

h That's a good idea! ....

i He's going to the USA next week. ....

1 use **a** to talk about one of something

2 use **an** to talk about one of something that begins with a vowel

3 use **the** to talk about one special thing that everybody knows

4 use **the** to talk about something for the second time

5 use **the** to talk about something when people know which one you are talking about

6 use **the** before the name of some countries

The first conditional

If	it	rains,	I'	will ('ll)	get wet.
	you	don't hurry,	you		be late.

Use **if** sentences to talk about things that will probably happen if something else happens.
Use the **present simple** in the 'if' clause, and **will** for the 'might happen' clause.

     If it **rains,** I'll get wet.

     If my brother **wins** the race, I'll be very happy.

We can change the order of the clauses:

     I'll get wet **if** it **rains.**

     I'll be very happy **if** my brother **wins** the race.

Use **do not / does not (don't / doesn't)** and **will not (won't)** to make negative conditional sentences.

     If he **doesn't** arrive soon, we'll be late.

     We **won't** arrive on time if you **don't** hurry.

I	will ('ll)	get wet	if	it	rains.
You		be late		you	don't hurry.

· ·

1   Match the two parts of these sentences.

a If it rains on Saturday,

b I'll be really happy if

c If the children are feeling better,

d If there are noises,

e If you are lying down,

f It will wake you up

g You won't be able to sleep if

h I won't take you to the movie

1 we'll come to the party.

2 you do vigorous exercise before you go to bed.

3 you'll have no problem falling asleep.

4 we'll stay at home.

5 if you don't finish your homework.

6 my cold is gone by tomorrow.

7 if the temperature goes above 24°C.

8 you'll find it difficult to sleep.

a ....
b ....
c ....
d ....
e ....
f ....
g ....
h ....

2 Complete the following sentences with the verb in brackets in the correct tense.

a If you .... (not lie down), you .... (not be able to) sleep.

b Your leg .... (get) better if you .... (rest).

c If you .... (study) hard, you .... (pass) the test.

d You .... (feel) better if you .... (drink) more water every day.

e Your heart .... (not get) stronger if you .... (not exercise) more.

f If I .... (eat) more calcium, ... my bones .... (get) stronger?

g You'll .... (catch) a cold if you .... (go out) in this rain.

h Will you .... (help) me with my homework if I .... (wash) the dishes?

i If you .... (listen to) that loud music, you .... (hurt) your ears.

j Will she .... (go) on holiday if she .... (not finish) the report?

3 Complete these sentences about yourself.

a If it rains this weekend, ...

b I'll do some exercise if ....

c If I pass this English course, ...

d If I ever win a lot of money, ...

4 Read these sentences from advertisements and complete them with the correct verb tenses.

a If you ...... *like* ...... (like) chocolate, you ...... *will love* ...... (love) our new chocolate chew bar.

b You .... (have) whiter teeth if you .... (use) our new toothpaste.

c Your clothes .... (stay) cleaner longer if you .... (wash) them with Brite washing powder.

d If your child .... (be) over three years old, she or he .... (enjoy) playing with the Shape Game.

e You .... (not be) sorry if you .... (change) to the Best Bank.

f If you .... (not have) time to eat, our new soup .... (fill) you up and .... (save) you time.

5 Now write the letter of the sentence from exercise 4 under the correct picture.

1 .c....

2 ....

3 ....

4 ....

5 ....

6 ....

6 Write sentences for these advertisements using first conditional.

....

....

....

....

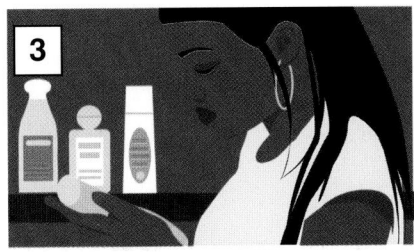

....

....

....

....

The zero conditional

If	ice	gets	warm,	it	melts.
	something	is	funny,	I	(always) laugh.

Use **if** sentences to talk abut things that are always true if something else happens. Use the **present simple** in the 'if' clause and in the 'something else happens' clause.

     If ice **gets** warm, it **melts**.

     If something **is** funny, I always **laugh**.

We can change the order of the clauses.

     Ice **melts** if it **gets** warm.

     I always **laugh** if something **is** funny.

Use **do / does not (don't / doesn't)** or **is not / are not (isn't / aren't)** to make negative zero conditional sentences.

     If ice **doesn't** get warm, it **doesn't** melt.

     I **don't** laugh if something **isn't** funny.

Ice	melts	if	it	gets	warm.
I	always laugh		something	is	funny.

1 Match sentences 1 and 2 with (a) or (b). Write 1 or 2 in the boxes.

1 If I exercise too much, I'll get out of breath.
2 If I exercise too much, I get out of breath.

a something that is always true. ☐
b something that is possible or probable. ☐

2 Read these sentences. Write T (true) if they tell you about something that is always true, or P (possible / probable) if they tell you about something that is possible or probable in the future.

a If you don't lie down, you won't fall asleep. ☐

b If you are at an altitude of over 4,000 feet, you need to breathe differently. ☐

c I always find it difficult to sleep if I drink coffee before I go to bed. ☐

d If you drink that coffee, you won't be able to get to sleep. ☐

e If you melt ice, it becomes water. ☐

f If you want some dessert, you'll have to eat your dinner. ☐

g If he doesn't study harder, he won't pass his exam. ☐

3 Match the two parts of these sentences.

a If you don't get enough sleep,	**1** I feel sick, because I'm allergic to them.
b You won't be able to do well in your exam	**2** you sleep to the sound of water.
c If I eat mushrooms,	**3** you'll feel tired for your exam.
d You always get tired	**4** if you don't eat properly.
e If you live near a river,	**5** it expands (gets bigger).
f If metal is heated,	**6** if you run more than five miles.

a .... b .... c .... d .... e .... f ....

4 Complete these sentences about yourself.

a If I eat too much,

....

b If I don't get enough sleep,

....

c If I study hard for this course,

....

d If it rains this weekend,

....

5 Read this article and circle the best way to complete these sentences.

a You will damage your hair if
   1 you don't eat enough iron.
   2 you eat vegetables.
   3 you eat too much meat.

b If you eat plenty of vitamin C,
   1 you must not eat fruits and vegetables.
   2 your hair will shine.
   3 your hair won't be healthy.

c If you cut your hair regularly,
   1 it will become thicker.
   2 it will become stronger.
   3 it will be easier to take care of.

d If you use hair products,
   1 it never damages your hair.
   2 you must be careful.
   3 they will never colour your hair.

Healthy Hair

Here are some tips for men and women to keep your hair healthy. You need to have enough iron in your diet. If not, you will damage your hair. Your hair stays healthy when you eat foods like meat, eggs, cereals, and vegetables like spinach.

First, to make your hair healthy and shiny, you must eat fruits and vegetables that contain vitamin C. Secondly, it is a good idea to cut your hair regularly. It does not become thicker or stronger when it is cut, but cutting your hair makes it easier to take care of.

Thirdly, be careful with the products that you use on your hair. When you colour your hair you can damage it. Some people have more delicate hair, so you should test a new product before you use it to see what happens to your hair. If it is hurt by a product or if your skin is allergic to a hair product, you must stop using that product to stop the problem from getting worse.

Countable & uncountable nouns

Countable nouns are nouns we can count. We can make them plural.

a **car** – two **cars** – four **cars**

a **potato** – two **potatoes** – twenty **potatoes**

Uncountable nouns are nouns we can't count because they are about something in general. We can't make them plural.

The **furniture** in her house is very old.

I like **rice**.

Some nouns have one meaning which is uncountable and another meaning which is countable

He loves **chocolate**. (= chocolate in general: uncountable)

He ate two **chocolates** from the box. (= little bits of chocolate: countable)

1 **Complete the table with the nouns in the sentences.**

Countable nouns (C)	a potato – three potatoes
Uncountable nouns (U)	milk
Countable and uncountable nouns	coffee – a coffee - coffees

a Vegetarians don't eat **meat**.

b I had **fish** for lunch.

c **Oranges**, **apples** and **bananas** are all **fruit**.

d I love tropical **fruits**.

e **Sugar** is bad for you.

f **Crisps** have a lot of salt.

g Is **stress** a serious **problem**?

h I bought **salad** and a box of **chocolates**.

i There is a wide variety of **salads** in this cafeteria.

j I love **chocolate**. I bought a box of chocolates.

2 Read this leaflet. Write the nouns in green in the correct place in the table in exercise 1 on page 24.

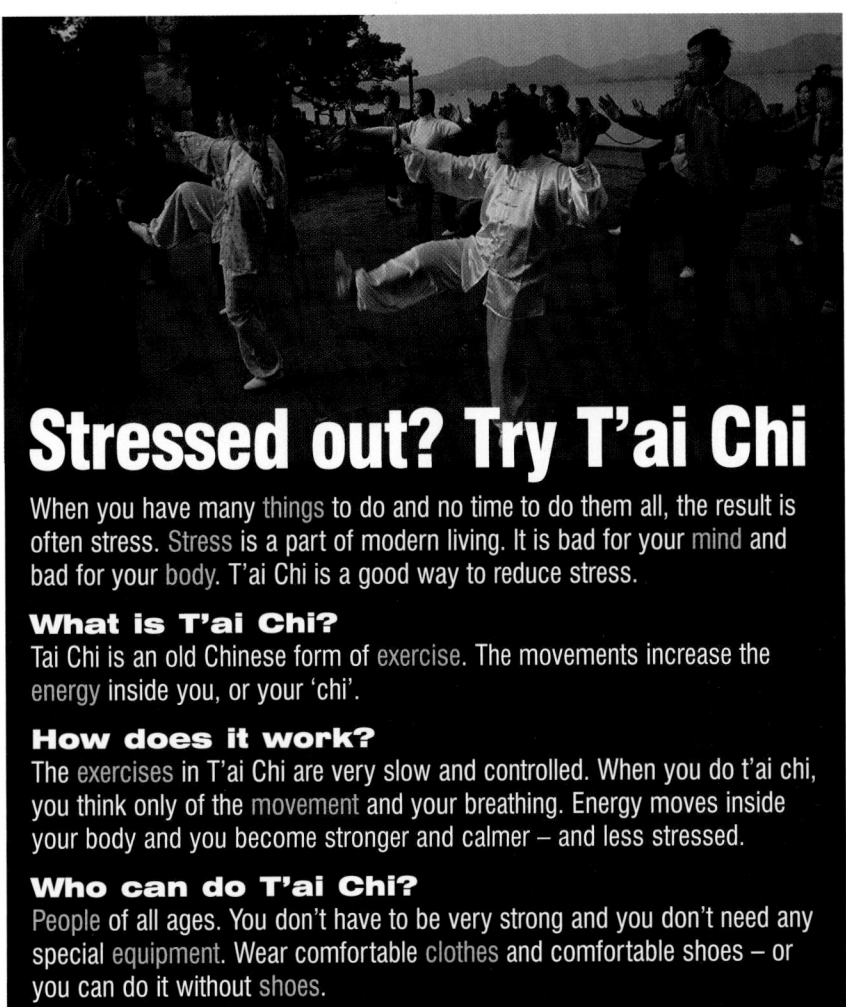

Stressed out? Try T'ai Chi

When you have many things to do and no time to do them all, the result is often stress. Stress is a part of modern living. It is bad for your mind and bad for your body. T'ai Chi is a good way to reduce stress.

What is T'ai Chi?
Tai Chi is an old Chinese form of exercise. The movements increase the energy inside you, or your 'chi'.

How does it work?
The exercises in T'ai Chi are very slow and controlled. When you do t'ai chi, you think only of the movement and your breathing. Energy moves inside your body and you become stronger and calmer – and less stressed.

Who can do T'ai Chi?
People of all ages. You don't have to be very strong and you don't need any special equipment. Wear comfortable clothes and comfortable shoes – or you can do it without shoes.

3 Label the nouns in the text C (countable) or U (uncountable).

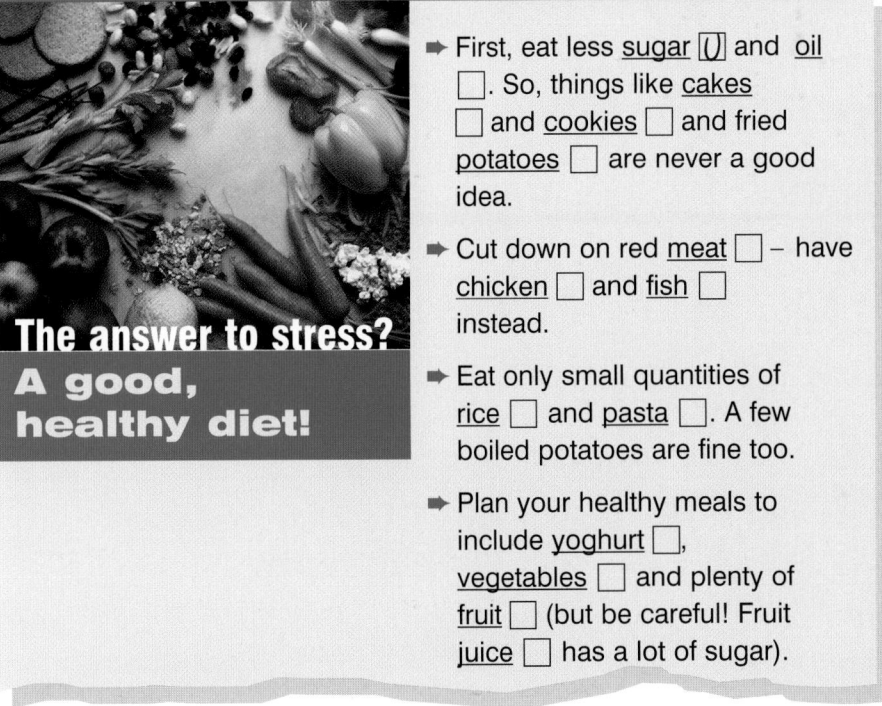

The answer to stress?
A good, healthy diet!

➡ First, eat less <u>sugar</u> ⊍ and <u>oil</u> ☐. So, things like <u>cakes</u> ☐ and <u>cookies</u> ☐ and fried <u>potatoes</u> ☐ are never a good idea.

➡ Cut down on red <u>meat</u> ☐ – have <u>chicken</u> ☐ and <u>fish</u> ☐ instead.

➡ Eat only small quantities of <u>rice</u> ☐ and <u>pasta</u> ☐. A few boiled potatoes are fine too.

➡ Plan your healthy meals to include <u>yoghurt</u> ☐, <u>vegetables</u> ☐ and plenty of <u>fruit</u> ☐ (but be careful! Fruit <u>juice</u> ☐ has a lot of sugar).

4 Write *a* or *an* before the nouns, where possible.

a ...*a*....... shoe   d .... stress   g .... orange

b .... exercise   e .... clothes   h .... furniture

c .... chicken   f .... equipment   i .... fish

5 Write the plural form of the nouns, where possible. If it is not possible, write NP.

a advice ....

b cheese ....

c paper ....

d furniture ....

e information ....

f homework ....

g milk ....

h apple ....

i rice ....

6 Circle the nouns that can be countable <u>and</u> uncountable.

salad   soup   stress   coffee   cake   fruit   chocolate   butter   clothing

Noun quantifiers

Use **a lot of** (or **lots of** – informal) with countable and uncountable nouns.

I need **a lot of** milk.

He bought **lots of** eggs at the farm.

Use **many** to talk about plural nouns in questions and negative sentences.

How **many** potatoes do you want?

Use **much** to talk about uncountable nouns in questions and negative sentences.

I haven't got **much** time.

How **much** money do we need?

Use **some** in positive and negative statements with plural nouns.

There are **some** pens in the drawer.

Some people just don't listen.

Use **some** in positive statements with uncountable nouns.

I'd like **some** milk in my coffee please.

Use **some** in offers and requests with uncountable and countable nouns.

Can you give me **some** advice?

Would you like to buy **some** socks?

Use **any** with countable and uncountable nouns in questions and negative sentences.

I don't want **any** sugar.

Have you got **any** apples?

1 Match the columns. The first one is done for you.

A little	———>	30 grams of butter
A few		24 eggs
Lots of		0 millilitres of milk
A lot of		4 tomatoes
No		1 kilo of cheese
No		0 potatoes

	Countable nouns	Uncountable nouns
Large quantities	a lot of	lots of
Small quantities	some	
No quantity	no	

2 Complete the table with phrases from exercise 1.

3 Complete the sentences with as many words and phrases from the table as possible.

a This hot chocolate is very, very sweet so don't put .... sugar in it.

b I love that shop. They have .... great cakes.

c .... people are learning to cook these days.

d This dish has .... butter and .... cream at all.

e .... recipes from this book, about three, are from India.

f .... people know this recipe, only some people in my family.

g Is there .... milk? I don't like black coffee.

h Are there .... cookies? I'd like some with my tea.

4 Complete the sentences with phrases from the table in exercise 2.

a For this recipe you need .... tomatoes, not .... , just two or three.

b You also need .... chicken, say 200 grams.

c Then you need .... olive oil. Not .... , about two tablespoons.

d Next, you need .... bread – two slices.

e .... salad is nice – a leaf or two.

f You can also add .... cheese. Just .... small pieces.

5 Can you guess what the recipe is? Check your guess at the bottom of the page.

6 Circle the right words. Decide first whether the nouns are countable or uncountable.

a I haven't got (much / many) free time during the week but at the weekend I have .... (many / lots of) time to see my friends.

b I have .... (much / many) friends, but only .... (a few / a little) good friends.

c We have to go shopping: there isn't .... (many / much) food in the fridge and there is .... (any / no) milk at all.

d Is there .... (any / some) coffee? Yes, but we haven't got .... (some / any) sugar.

e In the past, I had .... (a few / not many) problems sleeping. Now I haven't got .... (some / any) and I feel great!

A chicken sandwich

-ing nouns (gerunds)

Use gerunds (verb + -ing) to make activity and sport nouns.
I have never tried skiing.
Stamp collecting is a boring / enjoyable activity.

1 Write the verbs (from the box) which you can use with the nouns. Sometimes more than one is possible.

a books .... *collect, read* ....

b films ....

c football ....

d horses ....

e music ....

f shopping ....

g stamps ....

h bird watching .... 🗝

| collect go go to play read |
| listen to ride watch |

2 Label the pictures with the names of the sports. Which two sports are not Olympic sports?

| bowling ~~cycling~~ fencing life-saving |
| pistol shooting running show jumping |
| swimming weightlifting |

a *cycling* ....

b ....

c ....

d ....

e ....

f ....

g ....

h ....

i ....

🗝

3 Which five sports in exercise 2 are part of a pentathlon? Complete the text with the names of sports.

The Pentathlon

The modern pentathlon is an Olympic sport. It consists of competition in five events in one day:

(a) .... (4.5 millimetre air pistol),

(b) .... (free style – 200 metres),

(c) .... (cross country – 3 kilometres),

(d) .... (jumping over low walls and other obstacles) and

(e) .... (indoor on a 18 x 2 metre piste using swords).

- -

4 Complete the sentences with an -ing form,

a I don't like ..... *playing* .... football. It's too exhausting!

b I like bird- .... , but I don't go when it's very cold.

c I like horse .... because I've always liked horses, and I love the exercise.

d I love .... books on holiday. Sometimes I finish six or seven!

e I've always been interested in stamp .... I've got a stamp from 1792 which is very, very valuable.

f If I feel bad, I .... shopping. It makes me happy.

g My favourite activity? Sitting by the fire, ... beautiful music.

- -

5 Make the verbs into -ing nouns to complete the sentences.

a I love (watch) .... *watching* .... the Olympic Games on television.

b I need to go (shop) .... for food.

c (smoke) .... is bad for you so don't even start!

d (swim) .... in the sea is usually fun.

e Do you enjoy (buy) .... clothes?

f What do you think about (box) .... for women?

Prepositions of place

Use **prepositions** before nouns to say where something is.
The bank is **opposite** the cinema.
She is **in front of** me.

1 Choose a word or phrase from the box to complete each sentence.
Use each word or phrase once only.

> above behind below between in
> in front of inside on top of next to
> opposite outside under

a The Just Films building is .... a church and a supermarket.

b The Just Films building is .... Dover Street.

c The Just Films building is .... the supermarket.

d The Just Films building is .... the station.

e The car park is .... the Just Films building.

f The film star is .... the Just Films building.

g The third floor of the Just Films building is .... the second floor and .... the fourth floor.

h There are a lot of photographers .... the entrance.

i There is a limousine .... the Just Films building.

j There's a helicopter .... the Just Films building.

k There's a tunnel .... Dover Street.

2 Look at words and phrases that are used with *at*, *in* or both (when talking about place). Complete the task which follows.

at	*in*	*at* or *in*
... the bus stop	... Turkey	... the cinema
... the entrance to the station	... the living room	... Steve's house
... home	... the office	... (the) hospital
... work		... the station
		... a café

3 Look at the pictures. Write where the people are.

a Steve   Jack

b Lucy

c Arrivals   Departures   Di

d Bus Stop   Judy

Jack is at Steve's house.

e Roger

f Pat

g Jim

h STATION   Vince

i John

j Hazel

4 Where is the ball? Use one of these prepositions to say where the ball is in relation to the table(s).

6 Write as many sentences about this picture as you can.

above	behind	between	on top of	next to	~~under~~

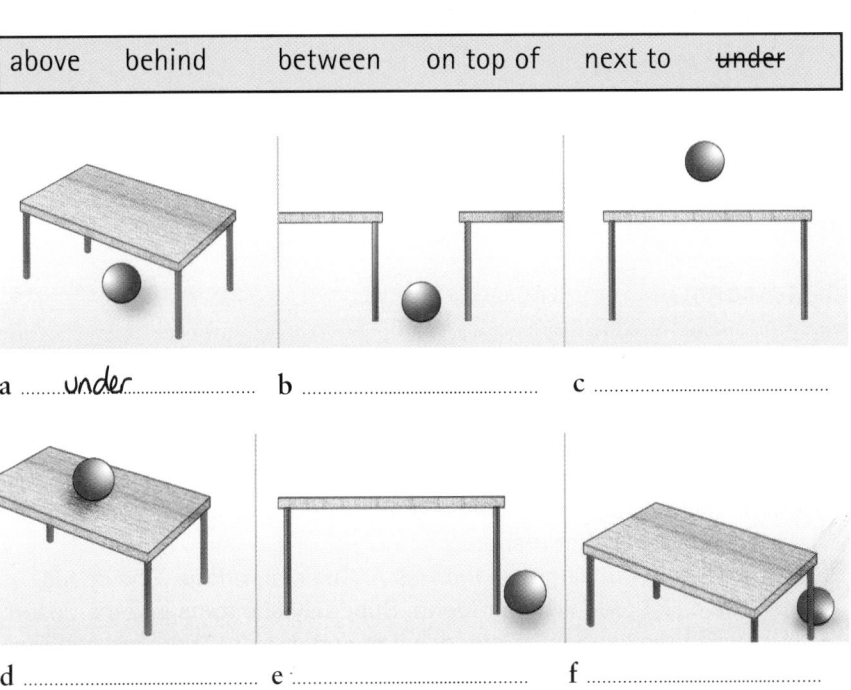

a ....under............   b ....   c ....

d ....   e ....   f ....

5 Now complete these sentences about this picture.

a The computer is inside ....

b .... is opposite the door.

c The cap is outside ....

d There is .... inside a box.

e Below .... there is a desk.

f The chair is in front of ....

Prepositions of movement

Use **prepositions** to say where something is going.
He climbed **up** the ladder.
She was walking **towards** the hospital.

1 Read the description of the first minutes of a new film 'The Driver'. Write the correct order of the pictures.

1 .....picture h.....

2 ....

3 ....

4 ....

5 ....

6 ....

7 ....

8 ....

9 ....

10 ....

11 ....

12 ....

THE DRIVER

In the first scene Sally drives onto a ferry. In the second scene she is driving off the ferry at Jebel Ali. She drives towards the airport, and then through the new airport tunnel to Terminal 1. She goes into the terminal building and meets her friend.

Then we see her driving over the Ras Al Khaimah bridge. She drives along the coast road with her friend. Suddenly she turns into the desert. She drives up a sand dune and down the other side. There are two men and three camels waiting for them... .

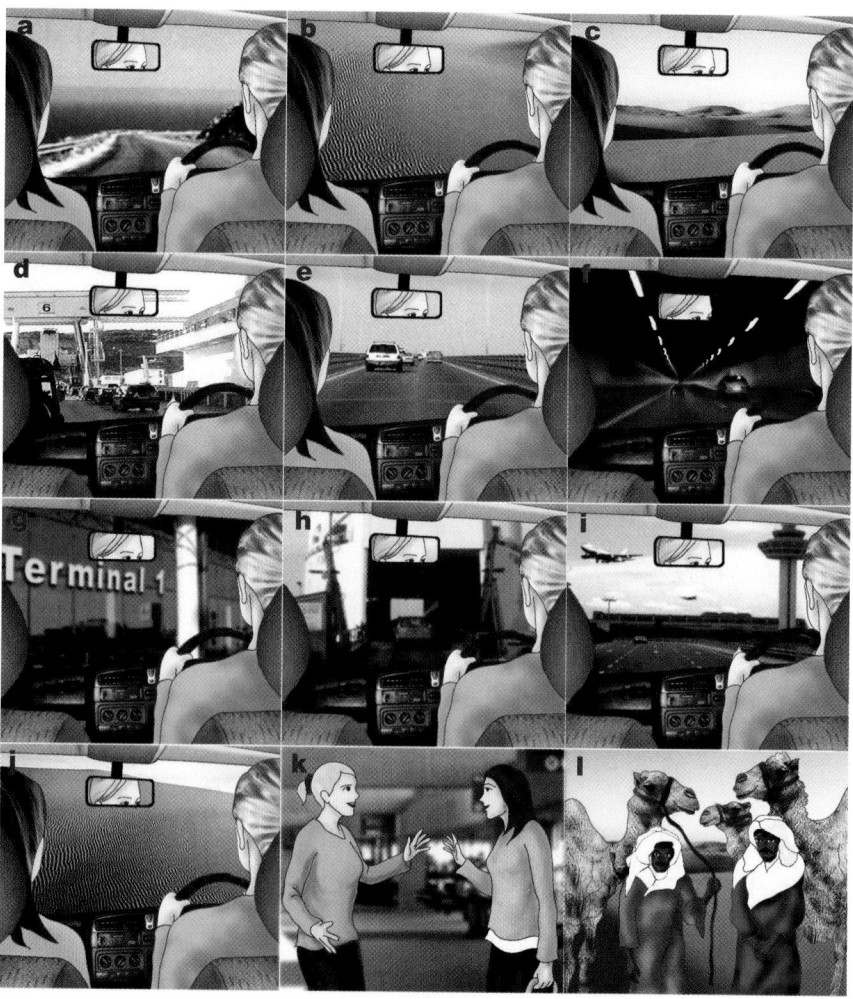

2 Read Mark's directions and draw a line to show the way to his house.

MARK: Walk along the road until you get to the bridge. Walk over the bridge and then turn left. Go down the hill towards the park. Go into the park and walk towards the lake. Turn right at the lake and walk towards the street. Turn right and walk down the hill. Turn onto Market Street and my house is the first house on the left.

3 Now draw a route to Katie's house and write how to get there.

The present simple

I You We They	(do not)	get up at 6.30 in the morning. play football on Sundays. watch TV in the evening.
He She It	(does not)	get(s) up at 6.30 in the morning. play(s) football on Sundays. watch(es) TV in the evening.

Use the **present simple** to talk about repeated actions and habits. Use -s when you talk about *he, she* or *it*.

       I **get** up at 6.30 every morning.

       She always **travels** to work by bus.

Use the present simple to talk about general facts that are true and will be for some time.

       We **live** in London.

       Ana **speaks** three languages.

Use the present simple to describe what happens in a story.

       Romeo **sees** Juliet at a big party.

       They **go** to Mexico on holiday.

Use **does not (doesn't)** for *he, she* & *it* and **do not (don't)** for *I, you, we, they* to make negative present simple sentences.

       I **don't** like TV programmes very much.

       He **doesn't** play the violin any more.

Do	you we they	play football?	Yes, I do. Yes, we do. Yes, they do.	No, I don't. No, we don't. No, they don't.
Does	he she it	watch TV?	Yes, he does. Yes, she does. Yes, it does.	No, she doesn't. No, she doesn't. No, it doesn't.

1 Read the sentences. Underline the verbs which are in the present simple.

   a She goes to school, she watches TV and goes shopping with her friends, but she doesn't eat well.

   b In game shows, people play games or answer questions and win prizes.

   c Most people buy magazines and watch TV.

   d Why do people like reality TV?

   e In the famous novel *Jane Eyre* (1847), Jane marries Mr Rochester.

2 Choose the correct form of the underlined verbs to complete the sentences.

   a I <u>cry</u> when I watch soap operas on TV. My mother .... too.

   b I <u>buy</u> magazines once a month, but my sister .... them every week.

   c My parents <u>watch</u> the news every night. My brother often .... with them.

   d In my house nobody <u>reads</u> the papers during the week, but we all .... them at the weekend.

   e We <u>don't</u> <u>have</u> a college newspaper. My friend's college .... one either. Maybe we can start one.

   f Our neighbours <u>have</u> many TV channels, but we .... only five.

   g We <u>have</u> a DVD recorder so I usually <u>record</u> my favourite documentaries. My grandmother .... one so I sometimes .... programmes for her.

3 Complete the questions.

   a What .... Kirsty .... to be? She wants to be a model.

   b What .... your younger sister .... with her pocket money? She buys books.

   c .... don't some girls .... well? Because they want to be thin.

   d .... some people want to be thin? Because they want to look like the models in magazines.

   e .... you .... TV? Every evening after dinner.

   f .... you .... listening to the radio? I love it! I can't do anything without music.

Presenting
Breakfast:
a dream job?

Breakfast is a programme on British television. The presenters
(a) ......interview...... (interview) people and (b) .... (read)
the news. Millions of viewers (c) .... (watch) it every
day.

Breakfast is on air live from 6.00 to 9.15 every morning. This
(d) .... (mean) a very early start for the presenters,
Dermot Murnaghan and Natasha Kaplinski. Natasha
(e) .... (get up) at 3.15. Dermot (f) .... (not
get up) so early but they both (g) .... (arrive) at the
studios at 4.30.

First they (h) .... (meet) with the producer of the
programme. Natasha and Dermot usually (i) ....
(interview) about 12 people every day so they (j) ....
(prepare) carefully – and fast! Then, they have to make sure
they look good.

So (k) .... they .... (enjoy) their job? 'It's
fantastic,' says Natasha. 'But the working hours are terrible'.
Natasha (l) .... (go) to bed at 8 o'clock and she
(m) .... (try) to go to sleep by 9.00. When does she
(n) .... (see) her friends? At lunchtime.
She (o) .... (not have) any other time!

So, do you think presenting *Breakfast* is a dream job?

4   Read the article. Fill in the
blanks with the present simple
of the verbs in brackets.

5   Write examples from the text for
each use of the present simple,
a, b and c.

a   We use the present simple to
talk about repeated actions
and habits.

...Natasha gets up at...
...3.15....
....

b   We use the present simple to
talk about general facts
which are true and will be for
some time.

....
....
....

c   We use the present simple to
describe what happens in a
film, book, television or radio
programme.

....
....
....

6 Interview Natasha. Write questions for the answers. Read the article again if you need to.

a YOU: What .... *is your job / do you do for a living* .... ?

NATASHA: I am a TV presenter. I present *Breakfast* with Dermot.

b YOU: What time .... ?

NATASHA: It starts at 6.00 and finishes at 9.15.

c YOU: What time .... ?

NATASHA: Very early. At 3.15!

d YOU: .... get up at 3.15 too?

NATASHA: No. He gets up a little later, but we start work at the same time.

e YOU: When .... ?

NATASHA: My friends? I see them at lunchtime – it's the only time I have!

f YOU: .... your job?

NATASHA: I love my job! But I don't really like the working hours.

7 Put the words in the correct order to write three more questions for Natasha.

a do / for / time / you / have / breakfast

.... *Do you have time for breakfast?* ....

b days / do / work / you / how many / week / a

....

c your family / what / think / about / does / working hours / your

....

d you / lots of / buy / new clothes / do / for work

....

The present simple: subject & object questions

Use object questions when you want to ask about the object of the verb.
Change the order of the words (subject and object).
Use **do / does** for the present simple and **did** for the past simple.
> He plays football. – What **does** he play?
> Tolstoy wrote *War and Peace*. – What **did** Tolstoy **write**?

Use subject questions when you want to ask who or what does or did something.
Don't change the order of the words (subject and verb).
> Tolstoy wrote *War and Peace*. – **Who** wrote *War and Peace*?
> Tanya is playing tennis with Jane. – **Who** is playing tennis with Jane?

1 Look at the pictures and answer the questions with the people in the box.

> Bart Simpson   'goody-goody' people
>
> Kenny's brother   Sally   Lola (the blonde girl)

1
a Who does Kenny love?
...... *Lola* ....
b Who loves Kenny?
....

2
a Who does Kenny admire?
....
b Who admires Kenny?
....

3
a What kind of people does Kenny dislike?
....
b What kind of people (probably) dislike Kenny?
....

2   Complete the table with examples from exercise 1.

Asking about the object: *Who / What* with **do** or **does**	Asking about the subject: *Who / What* without **do** or **does**
Who do you admire? Nicole Kidman. What programmes do you watch? (I watch) comedies and soap operas.	Who admires Nicole Kidman? I do. (I admire her). What makes you laugh? Comedies (do).

3   Read the sentences. Ask questions about the underlined sections, using the given question word. Write the answers using the underlined words.

a Everybody wants to be a millionaire. Who?

Q: Who wants to be a millionaire?

A: Everybody does.

b Everybody wants to be *a millionaire*. What?

Q: ....

A: ....

c Many people read magazines about celebrities. What?

Q: ....

A: ....

d Many people read magazines about celebrities. Who?

Q: ....

A: ....

e Celebrities don't like photographers. Who?

Q: ....

A: ....

f Celebrities don't like photographers. What?

Q: ....

A: ....

g Monkeys eat nuts and fruit. What?

Q: ....

A: ....

h Monkeys eat nuts and fruit. Who?

Q: ....

A: ....

4 Nancy and Norah are identical twins, but they are very different. Unscramble the lines and complete the sentences with Norah and / or Nancy.

a .....Nancy..... likes trees and flowers.

b .... admires Bono (and her sister does, too, secretly).

c .... reads romantic novels. .... reads her sister's diary (secretly!)

d .... watches soap operas and .... watches documentaries.

e .... loves Barry. .... does too.

f Does Barry love .... ? No. He only loves his rock band.

5 Complete the questions about Nancy and Norah. Use the verbs in brackets.

a What (like) .....does Nancy like..... ? Trees and flowers.

b Who (like) .... trees and flowers ? Nancy does.

c Who (love) .... Barry? Both girls do.

d Who (love) .... ? His rock band.

e What programmes (watch) .... ? Soap operas.

f Who (admire) .... Bono? Both girls do.

g Who (admire) .... Nancy? Norah does.

h What (read) .... ? Her sister's diary (secretly!)

i Who (watch) .... television? Both girls do.

The present continuous

I You We They	are	(not)	living in Switzerland. studying Turkish. doing homework. listening to music.
He She It	is		

Use the **present continuous** to talk about things in progress (= they have not finished).
Use **am / is / are +** verb **–ing**.

Ken's study**ing** Russian for a few weeks.
They**'re** stay**ing** at a friend's house this weekend.

Use **is not (isn't)** for **he, she** & **it**. Use **are not (aren't)** for **you, we, they**.
Use **am not ('m not)** for **I**.

She **isn't** enjoying her holidays.
We **aren't** living in London any more.

We also use the present continuous to talk about future plans and arrangements (see unit 18).

I'm seeing him tomorrow.
We're leaving on Tuesday.

Am	I			Yes, I am.		No, I'm not.
Are	you we they	reading a book? playing football?		Yes, you are. Yes, we are. Yes, they are.		No you aren't. No, we aren't. No, they aren't.
Is	he she it	watching TV?		Yes, he is. Yes, she is. Yes, it is.		No, she isn't. No, she isn't. No, it isn't.

1 You can use the present continuous to talk about the present [P], and to talk about the future [F].
Are the underlined verbs about the future or the present? Write P or F in the boxes.

a We <u>are playing</u> [ ] in the final on Sunday, so we<u>'re training</u> [ ] hard.

b I'<u>m meeting</u> [ ] my client tomorrow, so I'<u>m checking</u> [ ] the plans.

c I'<u>m practising</u> [ ] because I'<u>m taking</u> [ ] my driving test tomorrow.

d I'<u>m working</u> [ ] hard now, but on Saturday we <u>are having</u> [ ] a party!

2 Which meaning usually takes a time expression, present or future? ....

3 Complete the table with the time expressions in the list. You can use some of them with both future and present meaning.

Time expressions for the present	Time expressions for the future
now	tomorrow

now   tomorrow   today
at 8 o'clock   next week
on 25th May   on Tuesday
at this moment   this week
in the summer
Monday afternoon

Can you add more time expressions to the table?

For more on the present continuous for future, see Unit 18.

4 Read these four sentences. Which ones are about regular or habitual actions? Mark them R / H. Which are about temporary actions or actions happening at the moment of speaking? Mark them T.

a Tony lives with his parents. ☐   c What are you doing there? ☐

b Sonya is living in Liverpool. ☐   d What do you do there? ☐

5 Complete the sentences in the text below with the simple present or present continuous form of the verbs in brackets.

6 You interviewed Marco. Write questions for Marco's answers. Use the present simple or the present continuous.

a *What do you know about a chef's job?*

Well, I know it's hard!

b .... ?

A famous chef.

c ....
in college?

I'm training to be a chef.

d .... at the
moment?

In a restaurant.

e .... ?

I wash dishes and help the chef.

f .... ?

Because she is the best cook I know!

g .... ?

No, I'm not. But, who knows? Maybe one day I will write one.

When he was young, Marco's parents had a restaurant. He loved helping in the kitchen and by the age of 12 he was a pretty good cook. Now, Marco (a) .... (want) to be a chef – a famous chef. But he (b) .... (know) it is a hard job. At the moment, Marco (c) .... (train) to be a chef in college. To get experience (and a little money!) he (d) .... (work) in a restaurant at night. He (e) .... (not do) interesting jobs at the moment: he (f) .... (wash) dishes and (g) .... (prepare) things for the chef every day. How (h) .... he .... (feel) about it? 'It's only temporary,' he says. 'And it's all part of the training.' 'The best cook I know is my mother', Marco says. 'So I (i) .... (write) down all her secrets little by little. Maybe one day I'll write a book. But at the moment I (j) .... just .... (work) hard and (k) .... (learn) as much as I can.'

The future: *will* (predictions / unplanned decisions)

Use **will** to make predictions about the future (we can shorten **will** to '**ll**).
(See also *going to*, Unit 16.)

> I think Brazil **will** win the World Cup.
> She'**ll** probably be here in a few minutes.

Use **will** when you make sudden unplanned decisions.

> I'**ll** call back in a few minutes.
> It's OK, I'**ll** wash the dishes.

Ask questions by changing the order of **will** and the subject

> **Brazil will** win the World Cup. – **Will Brazil** win the World Cup?
> **I'll** wash the dishes. – **Will you** wash the dishes?

Use **will not** to make negative sentences (we can shorten **will not** to **won't**).

> I **won't** see you tomorrow.
> They **will not** win this game.

1 Look at these pictures. What are the missing words in the speech bubbles?

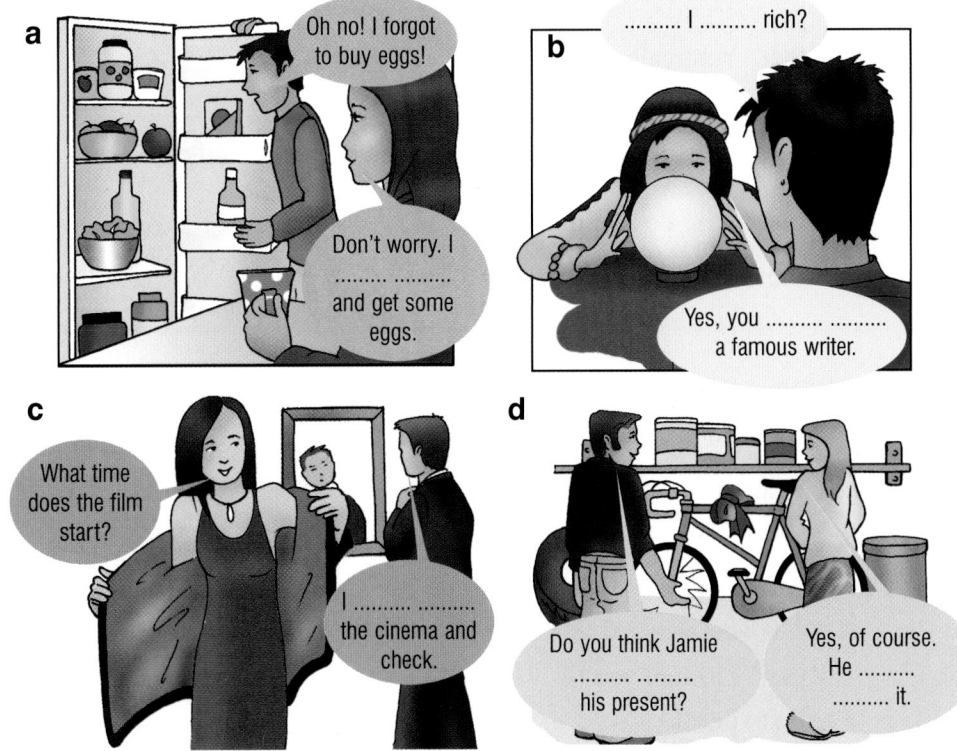

a Oh no! I forgot to buy eggs!

Don't worry. I .... and get some eggs.

b .... I .... rich?

Yes, you .... a famous writer.

c What time does the film start?

I .... the cinema and check.

d Do you think Jamie .... his present?

Yes, of course. He .... it.

2 Write the letters of the pictures in the boxes.

a These are predictions about the future. ☐ ☐

b These are decisions which have not been planned. ☐ ☐

3 Look at the phrases in bold. Which are predictions and which are unplanned decisions? Write P or UD.

JOHN: What do you think about the soccer game on Saturday?

MEL: Oh, I think **Chelsea will win.** (a) ....

JOHN: I'm not so sure. **Arsenal will give** them a hard time, I think. (b) ....

MEL: Do you think so? **I'll buy you lunch** if they win. (c) ....

JOHN: OK. It's a deal!

MADELINE: Hello. I'd like to speak to the manager, please.

RECEPTIONIST: I'm afraid she's not here at the moment.

MADELINE: **Will she be back later?** (d) ....

RECEPTIONIST: Yes, **she'll be in the office** by 2 o'clock. (e) ....

MADELINE: Thanks. **I'll call back then.** (f) ....

MUM: If you eat any more strawberries, **there won't be enough for tea.** (g) ....

RONNIE: But I like strawberries!

MUM: OK, you can eat those and **I'll buy some more for tea.** (h) ....

RONNIE: Thanks, mum. **I'll wash the dishes tonight.** (i) ....

MUM: You really do like strawberries!

4 Complete these dialogues with predictions or unplanned decisions, using the verb in brackets.

JODIE: Who do you think (a) .... (be) at the party?

MARTIN: Here's what I think. James (b) .... (be) there, because it's his party. Kristen (c) .... (go), because she doesn't like James, and Richard (d) .... (go) because he's sick.

JODIE: What do we have to take?

MARTIN: I don't know. I think I (e) .... (take) some crisps.

JODIE: That a good idea. I (f) .... (make) some dip to go with them.

LAURA: (g) .... I .... (make) a good doctor, mum?

MUM: I think you (h) .... (be) a great doctor, dear.

LAURA: I'm worried that I (i) .... (pass) all the exams.

MUM: I'm sure you (j) .... (do) very well in the exams.

LAURA: But (k) .... the teachers .... (be) helpful?

MUM: Yes, I think they (l) .... (be) helpful and you (m) .... (have to) study hard, but you (n) ....

5 Match what the person is saying to the pictures.

  a He won't be here. ☐   **c** I think you'll like this. ☐

  b I'll carry that for you. ☐   **d** I think I'll go for a walk. ☐

Which sentences are examples of predictions? ....

Which sentences are examples of unplanned decisions? ....

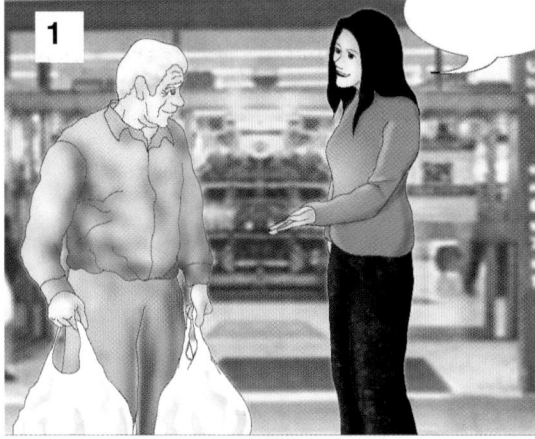

6 Complete this conversation with appropriate forms of the future simple.

RICHIE: Hey Emma! You know a lot about runners. Who

           (**a**) .... (win) the marathon on Saturday?

EMMA: Well, Mark Brown is the fastest man, so I think he

           (**b**) .... (get) first place.

RICHIE: What about Mike Harris? Do you think he

           (**c**) .... (come) second?

EMMA: No, he (**d**) .... (be) second. Fred Garrett is

           faster than he is. Fred (**e**) .... (beat) Mike Harris.

RICHIE: (**f**) .... the race .... (be) on TV, do you

           think?

EMMA: Oh, yes, I'm sure it (**g**) .... (be) on TV, but I

           (**h**) .... (be able) to watch it.

RICHIE: Why not?

EMMA: I (**i**) .... probably .... (have to) help my

           parents in their shop.

RICHIE: I (**j**) .... (record) it for you and you can watch it

           later.

EMMA: Thanks.

The future: *going to*

I You We They	am / are	going to	listen to some music. play football. read a book. watch TV.
He She It	is		

Use **going to** to talk about plans and intentions. **Going to** is followed by an **infinitive verb**.

> Next year I'm **going to study** Greek.

> I'm **going to watch** TV this evening.

Use **going to** to make predictions about the future (See also *will*, Unit 15.)

> I think next year is **going to** be fantastic.

> She's probably **going to** get here in about 30 minutes.

Use **is / are not going to** to make negative sentences (we can shorten **is not** and **are not** to **isn't** and **aren't**).

> I **am not going to** be late.

> He **isn't going to** travel to St Petersburg.

Am Are	I you we they	going to	read a book? play football? watch TV?
Is	he she it		

Yes, I am.	No, I'm not.
Yes, you are. Yes, we are. Yes, they are.	No, you aren't. No, we aren't. No, they aren't.
Yes, he is. Yes, she is. Yes, it is.	No, he isn't. No, she isn't. No, it isn't.

1 Look at these sentences about Jodie and write PAST if they refer to something that happened in the past, PRESENT if they refer to a situation in the present, or FUTURE if they refer to the future.

a Last year I went to France for a year. ....

b Next year I'm going to go to Russia to learn Russian. ....

c At the moment I'm studying French at night school. ....

d My family and I are going to buy a new house this year. ....

e I've never been to Russia before. ....

f My friends work in that school over there. ....

g I'm not going to be a teacher, I'm going to be a translator. ....

2 Read the conversation and complete it with the correct form of *going to*.

LAURA: So, what (**a**) *are you going to do* .... (do) this weekend, Frank?

FRANK: Well, (**b**) .... (go) to a party on Saturday.

LAURA: Great! Whose party?

FRANK: My uncle John (**c**) .... (get) married on Saturday and he and his wife (**d**) .... (have) a big reception in the evening.

LAURA: (**e**) .... (take) anyone with you?

FRANK: No, (**f**) .... (take) anyone.

LAURA: Oh.

FRANK: What (**g**) .... (do) on Saturday?

LAURA: Nothing. (**h**) .... (do) anything.

3 Look at these pictures and write what is going to happen.

a ~~They're going to have breakfast.~~

b ....

....

c ....

....

d ....

....

4 Read these situations. Are the sentences in bold true or false? Correct the sentences that are false.

a It has started to rain and Steve and Lisa don't have an umbrella.

They are not going to get wet.

~~False. They're going to get wet.~~

b David studies mathematics every day. He is very good at maths.

He's going to fail the mathematics exam.

....

c John and Emma are wearing skis.

They're going to go swimming.

....

d There are black clouds everywhere and it's cold.

It's going to rain.

....

e Richard and Charlie are sitting at their desks with their English textbooks open.

They're going to play video games.

....

f The film starts at 8.30 pm. Julia and Michael live twenty miles from the cinema. They are leaving their house at 8.15 pm.

They are going to be late for the film.

....

The future: plans & intentions

1 Complete these conversations. Use *will* or *going to*.

Conversation 1

MARTINA: What (**a**) .... you .... do in the summer?

CARL: Well, I think (**b**) I' .... be able to get a job at my uncle's shop.

MARTINA: (**c**) .... you .... go on holiday?

CARL: No, (**d**) I' .... save as much money as I can, because (**e**) Kevin and I .... spend six months in Australia next year.

MARTINA: That's great. (**f**) You' .... love it there. It's a great country.

Conversation 2

CANDY: Do you think (**g**) you' .... pass your final exams?

JIMMY: Well, (**h**) I' .... be really angry if I don't, because I've worked really hard this term. **i**) I' .... work for a top law firm.

CANDY: (**j**) .... you still get the job if you fail your exams?

JIMMY: Oh, (**k**) I .... fail my exams.

CANDY: It's good that you're so confident.

2 Which verbs in exercise 1 talk about planned intentions and which talk about predictions?

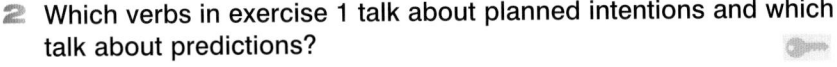

MONDAY	THURSDAY
Get to work early (meeting at 7 am)	Report for Helen (7 am)
Lunch with James Crawford 1 pm	Lunch with Helen
Gym 6 - 7	Gym 6 - 7 pm
Movies 8 pm	Dinner with Harry (8 pm)

TUESDAY	FRIDAY
Meeting at 8 am	Breakfast meeting 8 am
Lunch with client 12.30	Work Late (- 9 pm)
Karate class 7 - 8	Drinks with Sue and
Dinner with Sue 9 pm	Helen

WEDNESDAY	SATURDAY
Meeting at 8 am	
Lunch with mum	SUNDAY
Meeting 7 - 9 pm	
Jane's birthday party 10 pm	

3 Read Maria's schedule and in a notebook, make sentences about her future plans.

Example: *She's going to go to work early on Monday.*

Now make predictions about her weekend.

Example: *I think she'll sleep until 10 am on Saturday.*

4 Underline the best answer to complete these conversations.

a MANDY: What are you going to study?
   JEFF: *I will study / I'm going to study* law.

b MUM: What are you going to do tomorrow?
   MELISSA: I'm not sure yet. *I'll probably / I'm going to* stay at home.

c OLD MAN: Oh, these books are heavy.
   YOUNG WOMAN: Do you need help? *I'll / I'm going to* carry your books for you.
   OLD MAN: Thanks, dear.

d MARTHA: What *are you going to / will you* do in the holidays?
   PETE: *We're going to / We will go to* Spain.
   MARTHA: That's nice.

e MIKE: I don't know what to write. I have to write a letter.
   LISA: I have an idea. Give me that pen – *I'll / I'm going to* write the letter for you.
   MIKE: Thanks.

f DARREN: Right. Here's my plan. I'm not going to paint the house. *I'm going to get some painters to do it. / I'll paint the house.*
   LOUISE: That sounds great. *I'll help you / I'm going to help you*, if you like.
   DARREN: That would be great.

6 Complete the sentences with *going* to or *will*.

a Stop! You're going too fast. You're .... fall off your bike!

b Oh, dear. I can't do this English homework. I .... fail!

c Oh, it's not so hard! Come on, I .... help you.

d Which film do you think .... win the Oscar for Best Film?

e I .... watch TV tonight. I .... finish packing for the holiday.

f Where .... you .... go on holiday this year?

g To Mexico. We .... stay there for three weeks.

h I think I .... have the roast lamb. Does that come with vegetables?

i .... you .... go to the class party on Saturday night?

j I don't know. I .... decide on Saturday morning.

k I .... tell you a secret, but you mustn't tell anyone else.

l I .... tell anyone else, I promise.

5 Match responses 1 – 8 to the questions a – h.

a What are you going to do next weekend? [5]
b Who do you think will win the chess competition? [ ]
c Will you help me with my homework tonight? [ ]
d Do you know what's she's going to study? [ ]
e What's he going to be when he grows up? [ ]
f Can you help me with this maths problem? [ ]
g Who will be the next world soccer champion? [ ]
h Are you going to go to Dave's party? [ ]

1 Yes. I'll see you there.
2 Sorry, I can't. I'm going to go to the cinema with Charlie later.
3 I think Jane will beat Mike.
4 Sure. I'll read the problem and you tell me what you don't understand.
5 We're going to visit my grandmother.
6 It's going to be a tough competition, but I think Brazil will win.
7 He's going to be a firefighter.
8 Yes. She's going to study psychology.

The present continuous

We use the **present continuous** tense to talk about arrangements for the future.
The president **is arriving** at 6 o'clock.
They**'re going** to Australia next week.
Use time expressions with the present continuous to show future plans.
I'm seeing the doctor **tomorrow.**
She's appearing in a new play **next month.**

1 Read these sentences. Do they have future or present meanings? Write F (future) or
P (present) in the boxes.

a Are you still looking for a job? P

b Julie's taking a photography course
all week. ☐

c They're showing the same film at the cinema
again next week. ☐

d What are you doing under the table? ☐

e Are you enjoying your work? ☐

f I can't go out tonight. I'm babysitting my
baby sister. ☐

g Everybody's getting a job this summer. ☐

2 Write each sentence twice, once with present meaning and once with future meaning.
Use time expressions from the box.

at the moment   (later) tonight   (right) now
from Monday   next week   at present
this morning   this week

a We' re watching a DVD.
We're watching a DVD now. (present)
We're watching a DVD tonight. (future)

b I'm taking an English lesson.

c We are doing some grammar exercises.

d He's working on a new project.

e Are you working?

?

?

3 Write three fun things you are doing this week and three things you don't really want to do.

Examples: I'm having a party on Saturday.
I'm going to the dentist on Tuesday.

4 Look at Matthew's diary for the week. Write questions and answers.

Monday	meet Elena	Friday	go to bank, have lunch with Tania
Tuesday	go shopping (a.m.) go to cinema (p.m.)	Saturday	go swimming
Wednesday	walk Billie's dog, watch tennis	Sunday	go to Rob's party
Thursday	play badminton (a.m.) out with Chris (p.m.)		

a What is he going to do .... on Monday?
  He's going to meet Elena. / He's meeting Elena.

b .... on Tuesday?
  In the morning ....
  In the evening ....

c .... on Wednesday?
  First, ... Then
  ....

d .... on Thursday?
  .... in the morning,
  and ....

e .... on Friday?
  .... , then
  ....

f .... on the weekend?
  .... on Saturday, and
  .... on Sunday.

The present perfect simple

Use the **present perfect simple** to talk about things that started in the past and which are still true.
Use **have + past participle** for **I, you, we & they**, and **has + past participle** for **he, she & it**.
  I **have** always **loved** chocolate.
  He's never **won** a competition.
Use the present perfect to talk about something that happened in the past, but which is still important for the present.
  I've **bought** a new car.
  They've **arrived**!
Use **have not (haven't)** with **I, you, we & they**, and **has not (hasn't)** with **he, she & it** to make negative present perfect sentences.
  I **haven't** been to India.
  She **hasn't** called me.

Have you ever	acted in a play? climbed Mount Everest? met a famous person?	Yes, I have. No, I haven't (have not).

1 **Match the questions and answers in this online interview.**

a What unusual foods have you tried?
b What are your hobbies?
c When did you become a vegetarian?
d Which country did you like best?
e Can you tell us something about yourself?
f What countries have you visited?
g How long have you lived in London?
h When did you go there?

Q: **1** ....
A: My name is Nadia Burton. I'm 22 and I'm from London.

Q: **2** ....
A: I've lived in London all my life, but I have travelled to a lot of different countries and done a lot of interesting things.

Q: **3** ....
A I've visited most countries in Europe, except Sweden, Norway and Denmark. I really want to go there.

Q: **4** ....
A: My favourite country is the Czech Republic.

Q: **5** ....
A: I went there in 2004 and I loved it.

Q: **6** ....
A: I'm a travel agent, so travel is my job and my hobby. When I'm not travelling I like to cook. I love to try unusual food.

Q: **7** ....
A: I have eaten a lot of unusual fruits and vegetables like star fruit, but there are a lot of meats that I have never eaten, because I am a vegetarian.

Q: **8** ....
A: About five years ago. I haven't eaten meat for five years.

2 Complete these conversations with the present perfect or the simple past.

Conversation 1

MIKE: (a) .... you ever .... (eat) octopus?

LAURA: Yes, I (b) .... (try) it last year.

MIKE: (c) .... you .... (like) it?

LAURA: Yes, it (d) .... (be) delicious.

Conversation 2

CINDY: I (a) .... (see) a great movie last

night. It's called *Escape from the*

Edge. (b) .... you .... (see) it?

BRAD: No, I (c) .... (not be) to the cinema for a long time, but I

(d) .... (go)

to the theatre last week.

CINDY: Really? What (e) .... you

.... (see)?

BRAD: It (f) .... (be) a play called

A Merry Life.

3 Complete the sentences with the correct form of the verb in brackets.

a Oh no! My bag .... (go)! I .... (leave) it here a minute ago.

b Petra! I .... (not recognise) you! .... you .... (lose) weight?

c Yes, I .... (be) on a diet for the last few weeks.

d 'Can you help me with my English? I .... (forget) when to use the past simple, and when to use the present perfect.'

e 'Sorry, I can't. I .... (give up) English a year ago. I .... (forget) everything about grammar.'

f They .... (open) a new Internet cafe next to my flat last month. But I .... (not be) there yet.

g On holiday in France my French .... (improve) a lot. But now I'm back home it .... (get) worse again.

h I .... (fail) my driving test. I .... (feel) really upset this morning, but I .... (just speak) to the instructor about it and I feel a lot better now.

4 Make sentences. Use the past simple or the present perfect.

a you / hear / the news? The Prime Minister / resign.
....

b Long ago / the Egyptians / use / hieroglyphics / for communication.
....

c I / not see / you / for ages. You / be / away?
....

d I / just / come back / from Italy.
....

e Alexander Graham Bell / invent / the telephone.
....

f you / finish / reading / that book / yet?
....

g Yes, / I / lend / it / to Gavin / yesterday.
....

The present perfect with *since* & *for*

I You We They	have	(not)	lived in Paris played football enjoyed TV been to my friend's house listened to his music	since	2001. yesterday.
He She It	has	.		for	three years. five minutes.

Use **since** to talk about a **specific time** in the past.
  I haven't seen him **since Friday**.
  She's been in Greece **since January**.
Use **for** to talk about a **period of time**.
  They've lived in England **for three years**.
  I haven't had a coffee **for two hours**.

1 Read the information and complete the task which follows.

Carlton Joseph: fashion designer

Carlton Joseph is a fashion designer, but not just any fashion designer. He appears on television, he writes books, and he owns his own fashion house.

    Born in 1980, Carlton started designing clothes when he was eleven. His father owned a clothes store, and Carlton used to work there at the weekend. Then he did a design course at college.

    When he was 21 someone suggested doing a TV programme. He made his first show 'Carlton's clothes' in 2004, and he wrote his first book in the same year. Since then he has written four more. Carlton got married to TV producer Susan Mills in 2005.

    Three months ago Carlton started his new company. He called it 'Design: Carlton'.

    At work Carlton always wears black trousers and a black top, but at home – or when he goes out – he wears clothes with bright colours (red, blue and yellow). He is especially keen on new glasses – he buys a new pair every few weeks. "I like to look different every day," he says.

    Carlton started wearing glasses when he was twelve. He dyed his hair red when he was 18. It is still red, and this year, for the first time, he has grown a beard. "My wife likes it, that's why," is his explanation. But his beard is black!

Make sentences about Carlton with *since* or *for*.

a Carlton has been a fashion designer .... *since 1991* ....

b He's been a TV star ....

c He's had his own company ....

d He's been a writer ....

e He's worn glasses ....

f He's had a beard ....

g He's had red hair ....

h He's been married ....

2 **Complete these phrases with *for* or *since*.**

a I've known him .... *for* .... four years.

b We've lived here .... I was a child.

c She waited for him .... twenty-five minutes.

d They've been married .... 1988.

e It's been three years .... I last saw her.

f I haven't been here .... we were both ten years old.

g She has been so worried about it .... you told her.

3 **Write *for* or *since*.**

a I'm really hungry! I haven't eaten .... ages.

b I know. I haven't had anything to eat .... 7.00 am, either.

c Have you had that jacket .... long?

d I've had it .... last summer.

e I've known Nicola .... ten years.

f Really? That must be .... you were at secondary school, then.

g He played for Arsenal .... five years.

h But since 2005 he's played .... Juventus.

i We've had cable TV .... 1999.

j It's ten years .... my grandma died.

4 **Read this paragraph and answer the questions below.**

Hi! I'm Lydia Brown and I'm from London. I moved to Paris five years ago and I moved back to London three months ago. I'm an executive for a music company and I work long hours. I've worked in this job since 2000 and I love it. My hobbies are Capoeira and dancing. I started classical ballet when I was little and I also do modern dance. I've never tried tap dancing, but I have always wanted to, ever since I was a child.

a How long did Lydia live in Paris?
....
....

b How long has she lived in London?
....
....

c How long has she been doing her present job?
....
....

d How long has she studied classical ballet?
....
....

e How long has she wanted to try tap dancing?
....
....

The past simple

Use the **past simple** to talk about things in the past that are finished/completed. Use **-ed** at the end of the verb.

We play**ed** tennis yesterday afternoon.

She talk**ed** about football this morning.

Some 'irregular' verbs in the past simple tense do not have -ed endings.

I **met** John at a party last year.

They **saw** a film on TV last night.

Use **did not (didn't)** to make negative past simple sentences.

I **didn't** see Sarah at the party.

He **didn't** finish his exam on time.

I You He She It We You They	did some homework. listened to music. lived in Paris. read a book. studied Turkish. watched TV.

Did	I you he she it we you they	do some homework? listen to music? live in Paris? read a book? play football? study Turkish?

Yes, I Yes, you Yes, he Yes, she Yes, it Yes, we Yes, you Yes, they	did.

No, I No, you No, he No, she No, it No, we No, you No, they	didn't.

1 Write the base form of the verbs. The first one has been done for you.

a laughed ...*laugh*....   d wanted ....   g felt ....   j met ....   m wrote ....

b memorised ....   e forgot ....   h gave ....   k put ....

c repeated ....   f found ....   i had ....   l tried ....

2 Complete a – k with verbs in the correct form, from exercise 1.

I (a) ..*met*...... an old friend in the street. She (b) .... me her phone number. I didn't (c) .... it down but I (d) .... it and (e) .... it many times in my head. The next day I (f) .... to phone my friend but I couldn't remember the number. Luckily I (g) .... her in the phone book. She laughed. 'Of course you (h) .... the number. Why didn't you write it down? At school you always (i).................. a terrible memory', she said. I (j) .... silly. Did I really have a terrible memory then? Well, not any more! Now, where did I (k) .... my keys?

3 Complete the questions. Write the correct form of the verbs in brackets.

a What is your earliest memory of school? What
happened that day? (happen) Who ....
you .... ? (meet) What .... the
names of your first friends? (be) Who
.... your favourite teacher? (be)

b Can you ride a bicycle, use a tin opener, or use
a mobile phone? How long ago .... you
.... those things? (learn)

c Pick an important event in the history of your
country. When exactly .... the event
.... ? (happen) What .... the
people .... ? (do)

d When .... you last .... the phone
to call someone who is not a friend? (use)
Why .... you .... ? (phone)
What .... the phone number? (be)

5 Complete the questions about Sigmund Freud for these answers.

a Where _did the Freud family move to_ in 1860?
To Vienna.

b When .... ?
When he was four.

c Where ....
go to school?
In Vienna.

d When .... ?
In 1938.

e How many .... ?
Nine, including his older half-brothers.

f Who .... ?
Martha Bernays.

g When .... ?
In London, in 1939.

4 Complete the text with the simple past of the verbs in brackets.

Sigmund Freud

A very short biography

Sigmund Freud was born on May 6, 1856 in Freiberg (now Pribor, Slovakia). But he
(**a**) _did not live_ (not live) in Freiberg for long. When he (**b**) .... (be)
four, his family (**c**) .... (move) to Vienna, Austria.

He (**d**) .... (live) in Vienna most of his life. He moved to England in
1938, after the Nazi invasion.

Sigmund Freud (**e**) .... (have) two much older half-brothers (from his
father's first marriage) and seven brothers and sisters.

At 17, Freud (**f**) .... (start) university. He (**g**) .... (study)
medicine. He (**h**) .... (graduate) from the University of Vienna and
became a doctor. But he (**i**) .... (not like) medicine. He (**j**) ....
(be) interested in people with emotional problems.

In 1886, Freud (**k**) .... (marry) Martha Bernays. They had six children.

Freud worked with Josef Breuer. In 1895 they published a book, *Studies in
Hysteria*. It was about a 'talking cure' they (**l**) .... (use) with their patients.
It was the beginning of psychoanalysis.

Freud's work is still very important today.

Sigmund Freud (**m**) .... (die) in London in 1939.

The past continuous

I			living in Switzerland.
You	was		studying Turkish.
We	were		doing homework.
They		(not)	listening to music.
He			
She	was		
It			

Use the past continuous to talk about things which were 'in progress' at a particular time.
Use **was/were** + verb **–ing**.

> She **was** watching TV at half past eleven last night.
> They **were** living in Argentina last year.

Use **was not / were not** (**wasn't / weren't**) to make negative past continuous sentences.

> I **wasn't** listening to his conversation at that moment.
> I hope we **weren't** talking too loudly.

1 Complete Polly's story with the past continuous form of the verbs in the box.

work look up get have not help do

POLLY'S STORY

I am really angry with Laura. Last week we (**a**) .... a project together. We agreed to meet at my house on Thursday and we started to work as soon as she arrived.

Well, when we (**b**) .... her mobile rang. She made some excuse about helping her father at his shop, and left.

When she left I continued to work. But when Sarah saw her later, she (**c**) .... coffee with Joe! I was really angry! While I was (**d**) .... on our project, she (**e**) .... fun with Joe! And then she phoned on Sunday when I (**f**) .... things on the Internet, you know for the project, and she said, 'How is it going?' I just said, 'I don't want to work with you any more. Do your project with Joe.' And I hung up. So now we are not talking. And you know what the worst thing is? I got a C for my project – Laura and Joe got an A!

2 Past continuous or past simple? Complete Laura's story with the correct form of the verbs in the box.

not work hear hang up help write
not do ring talk arrive

LAURA'S STORY

Polly's not telling the truth. First of all, Polly and I (**a**) .... She was just messing around. We (**b**) .... anything important. It's true that my mobile (**c**) .... when we (**d**) .... Polly was furious! But it was dad, honest! So I did go and help him. I (**e**) .... in the shop when my brother (**f**) .... , so I left. I met Joe in the street and we had coffee together. What's the problem? I phoned her later but she (**g**) .... when she (**h**) .... my voice. So, fine, I did the project with Joe and she (**i**) .... hers alone. By the way, Joe and I did really well on our project!

3 Put the verbs in brackets in the correct form: the past simple or the past continuous.

a When Polly .... (hear) about Laura and Joe, she
.... (get) jealous.

b When Sarah .... (see) Laura, she .... (have) coffee
with Joe.

c While Laura .... (have) fun, Polly .... (work) on
their project.

d Polly and Laura .... (talk) when her dad .... (ring).

e What .... Laura .... (do) when her brother
.... (arrive)?

f Polly .... (get) angry when she .... (hear) about
Laura's coffee with Joe.

g Polly and Laura .... (not talk), so we .... (not
enjoy) the party much.

4 Copy these time lines. They represent time passing. Write the verbs in the sentences b – d above the lines like in a, and show how long the verb was happening.

a   When we *were working* at my house, her mobile *rang*.

were working
the past _____xxxxxxxx_____ now (the present)

the past _____x_____ now (the present)
rang

b   She *phoned* on Sunday when I *was looking up* things on the Internet.

the past _____x_____ now (the present)

the past _____xxxxxxxxx_____ now (the present)

c   I *was working* on our project while she *was having* fun with Joe.

the past _____xxxxxxxx_____ now (the present)

the past _____xxxxxxxx_____ now (the present)

d   We *started* to work as soon as she *arrived*.

the past _____xx_____ now (the present)

the past _____xx_____ now (the present)

5 Complete the sentences. Use the past continuous of the verbs in brackets.

Example: When the doorbell rang, I (have a shower).

When the doorbell rang, I was having a shower.

a When I fell off my bike, I (hurt my shoulder).

....

b When I saw them, they (hold hands).

....

c When I saw Melissa, she (go to the hairdresser's).

....

d At 8 o'clock yesterday evening, I (have dinner).

....

e When the teacher came into the classroom, I (send a text message).

....

f I saw her at the party last night, she (wear some new boots).

....

g When I saw him at the ticket office, he (buy tickets for the show).

....

h When we saw them at the club, they (dance).

....

6 Complete this story with the past continuous tense of the verbs in brackets.

A scary moment

It was a cold winter's night. It (**a**) .... (rain) but it was very windy. I (**b**) .... (sit) on the sofa watching a film on TV. It was really scary: a girl (**c**) .... (babysit) late at night. She (**d**) .... (watch) a film too. The phone rang and a man's voice said: 'Go check on the baby.' This happened several times. The girl ran to the baby's room: the baby wasn't there! It was a frightening film!

At that moment my phone rang. My heart raced, and my hands were sweating. I picked up the phone but all I heard were funny noises: some people (**e**) .... (talk), others (**f**) .... (laugh), someone (**g**) .... (scream). But nobody answered. I was so scared! A few minutes later I heard a noise: somebody (**h**) .... (try) to open the door!

But it was only my sister. She (**i**) .... (try) to open the door in the dark. I told her about the phone. She laughed. 'It was my mobile,' she said. 'I pressed your number by mistake and I only noticed as I (**j**) .... (park) the car. Sorry!'

The past continuous & past simple

1 Look at the picture carefully. What happened at seven o'clock yesterday morning? Choose the correct answer.

a A van crashed into a gorilla.
b A van crashed into another car.
c A gorilla escaped from a van.
d A gorilla went for breakfast.

2 Look at the picture again. What were the people doing at seven o'clock yesterday morning? Complete each sentence with the correct form of a verb from the box.

clean s stand s have breakfast s bring in s deliver s
walk (x2) s wait s read s jog

a A window cleaner ...... *was cleaning a shop window* ....

b A man .... his dog.

c A group of children .... to school.

d Three people .... for the bus.

e A boy .... newspapers on his bike.

f A man .... on the corner.

g A woman .... the milk.

h Two girls ....

i The baker .... outside the bakery.

j Some people .... in a café.

3 Use these words to make questions in the past continuous. Use capital letters where necessary.

a   window cleaner / do / what

   ....*What was the window cleaner doing?*............ ?

b   you / do / at 7 o'clock / yesterday morning

   .... ?

c   stand / the man / where

   .... ?

d   the people / wait for / what

   .... ?

e   the children / go / where

   .... ?

f   everybody / look at / what

   .... ?

g   the gorilla / walk / in the street / why

   .... ?

4 Cover the picture on page 64. Mark these sentences T (true) or F (false). Then correct the false statements.

a   The man at the corner was reading a book.

   ....*F He wasn't reading a book, he was reading a newspaper.*............

b   Everybody was looking at the gorilla.

   ....

c   A woman was bringing in the newspaper.

   ....

d   The children were riding their bikes to school.

   ....

e   The baker was standing outside his shop.

   ....

f   A man was walking a large dog.

   ....

g   The children were wearing jeans.

   ....

5 Read the article.
Complete the
sentences with the
correct form (past
simple or past
continuous) of the
verbs in brackets.

Horror in the city

It was a lovely morning. When I left the house the sun
(a) .... (shine) and I (b) ....
(feel) happy. But the feeling didn't last long.
When I (c) .... (arrive) at the station, lots of
people were waiting to buy a ticket. The man
(d) .... (close) his ticket window just as
I got there. 'Sorry. It's my tea break,' he said.

The train was leaving when I (e) ....
(get) to the platform. The next train was packed.
I (f) .... (stand) all the way while some
children sat comfortably. No one (g) ....
(offer) me a seat. Children are so impolite these days!

A woman was standing next to me. She
(h) .... (read) her paper when a child put his
hand in her bag. 'Thief!' I shouted. 'That boy is taking your
purse!' But the boy was the woman's son. Well, I (i) .... only ....
(try) to help.

When I left the station it (j) .... (rain). People were pushing and running.
When I got to the office, I certainly (k) .... (not smile) anymore.

6 Read the article again. Find sentences to match the patterns.

Past simple – happened
Past continuous – was happening

Pattern 1
Something was happening when something else happened.

a *The train was leaving when I got to the platform.*

b ....

c ....

Pattern 2
Something was happening while / when something else was happening.

d ....

Pattern 3
Two things happened at the same time.

e ....

7   Complete the questions with the correct form of the verbs in brackets, simple past or past continuous.

a   A: What ....*was*........ Brian........*doing*........when you ....? (do, arrive)

    B: He was washing his car.

    A: What .... he .... when you .... ? (do, arrive)

    B: He offered me a cup of tea.

b   A: What .... you .... when you .... the
        accident? (do, see)

    B: I was driving home.

    A: What .... you .... when you .... the
        accident? (do, see)

    B: I phoned for an ambulance.

c   A: What .... you .... about when the alarm clock
        .... ? (dream, ring)

    B: I was dreaming of you.

    A: What .... you .... when the alarm clock
        .... ? (do, ring)

    B: I threw it out of the window!

d   A: What .... your friend .... when you
        .... home? (watch, get)

    B: A football game.

    A: What .... you .... when you ....
        there? (watch, be)

    B: The same football game!

8   Correct the mistakes in the sentences. One verb in each sentence is in the wrong tense.

were cycling

Example: *When I saw you yesterday, you* ~~cycled~~ *home.*

a   She practises the piano when Jack came home.

b   When I was arriving, they were having tea.

c   I was revising for the English exam when you were ringing.

d   While I waited for the bus, there was a road accident.

e   When you saw me last night, I went to the bookshop.

f   When I saw them at the theatre, they had a drink at the bar.

used to

I You He She It We You They	used to	play tennis. live in a flat. go to work by bicycle.

Use **used to** to talk about repeated actions and feelings in someone's past life. **Used to** is followed by an **infinitive verb**.

We **used to** go to the cinema every Friday.
Buildings **used to** be smaller in those days.

I You He She It We You They	didn't	use to	play tennis. live in a flat. go to work by bicycle.

Use **did not (didn't)** to make negative **used to** sentences. <u>Don't</u> use the **–d** ending.
I **didn't use** to like TV, but now I do.
They **didn't use** to go to school.

Did	I you he she it we you they	use to	play tennis? live in a flat? go to work by bicycle?

Yes,	I you he she it we you they	did.

No,	I you he she it we you they	didn't.

Ask questions by using **Did** and **use to** (without -d). Change the order of the words.

We **used to** go to the cinema every Friday.
– **Did you use** to go to the cinema every Friday?
Buildings **used to** be smaller in those days.
– **Did buildings use** to be smaller in those days?

1 Read the quotes. How old is Mrs Hall – around 60, around 80 or around 100?

We didn't use to have a car. They were very new and very expensive!

We didn't have a phone. There used to be just one in our village – for emergencies.

When I was a child we used to play board games. There was no TV!

Girls didn't use to stay in school for very long. I left school when I was 12.

We used to watch a film occasionally. Films were silent then.

2 Read the quotes in exercise 1. Complete the table.

Talking about past habits:
Affirmative:
Negative:

3 Write the correct form of *used to* with the words in brackets to complete the sentences.

a The Halls .... (have) a family holiday at the beach every summer. Then the children grew up and everything changed.

b They .... (not go out often). But they had lots of fun. The whole family .... (play board games) together. Television changed all that.

c Mrs Hall loved the fashion in the 1950s. Women .... (wear fun clothes) and .... (have interesting hairstyles). Mrs Hall .... (love dancing) rock and roll. She is too old to dance now.

d In the 1960s, Mrs Hall got her first car. She .... (not drive) before that.

4 Write sentences from this paragraph under the correct headings.

Believe it or not, I used to play in a rock band! We used to play at parties and clubs. Then I got married so I left the band. I used to miss playing, terribly. But I don't anymore. Now, I usually play my guitar just at family parties.

Past habits

a ....

....

b ....

....

c ....

Present habits

d ....

....

Completed actions

e ....

....

5 Put the words and phrases in the correct order to make sentences about fashions. Add *used to* or *didn't use to* in the correct places, and put in any necessary capital letters.

Did you know?

a until the 1960s / British businessmen / wear / bowler hats /
British businessmen used to wear bowler hats until the 1960s.

b some ancient Romans / wash / very often / their hair / they / on 13 August, / it / only / wash / the birthday of the goddess Diana /

....

c their worst enemy / the ancient Egyptians / the picture of / paint / inside their sandals /

....

d in the 1970s / egg, butter or toothpaste / punks / in their hair / put / they / painted it / with food colouring or spray paint / then /

....

e in the 19th century / very tight corsets / women / wear / to look thin / faint / some women / or break their ribs /

....

6 Ask questions about the fashions in exercise 5. Use the correct form of *used to*.

a What ....*did British businessmen use to wear*.... ?
Bowler hats.

b How often .... ?
Only once a year!

c Why .... ?
Because then they could walk on them all the time, I suppose.

d When .... ?
On 13 August, the birthday of the goddess Diana.

e Why .... ?
Because their corsets were too tight.

Modal verbs: *can & can't*

Use **can** and **can't** to talk about abilities (= things we are (not) able to do because we are strong, clever, or have learnt them).

> She **can** speak Turkish.
> He **can't** run very fast.

Use **can** and **can't** to say when something is (not) possible.

> I **can** see you at 11 o'clock tomorrow.
> We **can't** connect to the Internet from this computer.

Use **can** in questions to ask someone to do something for you.

> **Can** you open the window?
> **Can** you help me with my homework?

Can May Might Will	I you he she it we you they	come this evening? play in the football team? pass the exam?	Yes,	I you he she it we you they	can. may. might. will.	No,	I you he she it we you they	can't. might not. won't.

Use modal verbs without another auxiliary verb to make yes / no questions.
Change the order of the words.

> I **could** play the guitar when I was six. – **Could you** play the guitar when you were six?
> I'll see you tomorrow. – **Will I** see you tomorrow?

For open questions use words like **when, what, how often**, etc.

> **When** will I see you?
> **What** could you do when you were little?

1 Circle the correct answer.

a *Can / Could* you swim when you were four years old?

b *Can / Could* you speak English when you were eight years old?

c Sorry, I'm busy, so *I can't /couldn't* come out with you tonight.

d Watch out! *Can't / Couldn't* you see that car is coming really fast around the corner?!

e I'm afraid I *can / can't* help you.

2 Complete the table with sentences a – g.

a We can meet outside the library.

b Can you bring your laptop with you?

c I can't come to the phone right now.

d I can't put a photograph into my computer document – they didn't show me how!

e Can you print photos from your computer?

f I can't read this document – it's in Swahili and I don't speak Swahili.

g Can you play the viola?

Use *can*	Examples
1 to talk about abilities or things people (don't) know how to do	
2 to say (or ask) if something is possible	
3 to ask someone to do something	

3 Match the sentences with the meanings.

a Abilities	1 Can you meet me after class?
b Know how to	2 Can you print this for me, please?
c Possibility	3 Can you use this software?
d Request	4 Can you type without looking at the keyboard?

4 Rewrite these sentences using *can* or *can't*.

a With this software it is possible to design posters, but it is not possible to make them in colour.

With this software you can design posters, but you can't make them in colour.

b Do you know how to download music from the Internet?

....

.... ?

c Please help me with this program.

....

.... ?

d Is it possible to take photos with this mobile?

....

.... ?

e Rizwan is good at taking photos of plants.

....

....

f I know how to fix a computer quickly.

....

....

g Howa is definitely not good at mixing music.

....

....

h Please take the CD out of the machine.

....

.... ?

Modal verbs: *could* & *managed to*

Use **could** to talk about ability in the past.
  I **could** speak Italian when I was four, but I can't now.
Use **could not (couldn't)** to talk about things people were unable to do.
  We **couldn't** understand a word when he spoke to us yesterday.
Use **managed to** to talk about things you could do in the end, but which were difficult.
  I **managed to** finish the test, but it was difficult.
Use **did not (didn't)** to make negative 'managed to' sentences.
  I **didn't manage to** do my homework last night.

1 Use *could*, *couldn't*, *managed to*, or *didn't manage to* to complete the sentences.

a Jon wanted a new TV. He .... save enough money to buy one with a plasma screen. He is very proud of his new TV.

b At the age of five, Rachel .... use a word processor and she .... play computer games. But at the age of 12 she .... multiply or divide without a calculator.

c Matthew .... understand what the problem was with his email. He .... get through to the helpline only after trying for hours.

d Mia's computer crashed but she .... to save most of her documents. Unfortunately, she .... save her address book so she .... write to her friends.

e Martha worked very hard, but she .... to pass her exam. It was surprising because in the past she .... always pass exams easily.

2 Complete the sentences about Pei-ling. Use *could*, *couldn't*, *managed to* or *didn't manage to* to complete the sentence. (Pei-ling is from Taiwan.)

a At the age of four she .... read the newspaper.

b At the age of six she .... record programmes from the television.

c At the age of eight she .... speak English well and she .... understand texts in Spanish.

d By the end of primary school she .... do algebra (but she .... ride a bike!).

e In secondary school she .... skip a year at school.

f At 13 she .... beat adults at chess and she .... win an international chess competition.

g Last year she .... pass her university entrance exams, but she still .... ride a bike.

3 Mark the sentences 1 or 2, depending on their meaning.

Meanings
1 talking about abilities in the past
2 talking about things that were difficult to do but which, once, you did

a Jim could climb up palm trees when he was young. ......**1**........
b Kris managed to open a window and got into the house. ....
c Did you manage to solve the puzzle? ....
d They couldn't fix Maria's MP3 player. ....

4 Read the text. Underline the correct verbs.

5 Complete the sentences. Use *could*, *couldn't*, *managed to* or *didn't manage to*.

a Last night I finally ...**managed to**... get to Level 6 of this game!

b .... you use a computer when you were 10?

c When Kevin was at school, he .... spell, but now he can.

d I phoned Jean lots of times, but I .... speak to her. She's never in!

e Irene lost some computer files and she .... get them back.

f She .... type with her eyes shut in those days.

g Vanessa .... understand the instructions at all.

h Did they .... install the new software?

i Can you believe it? Johnny .... repair watches when he was five!

Kids these days can do things I (**a**) *could / couldn't / managed to / didn't manage to* do at their age. Some things I still can't do. I feel a bit silly sometimes.

Yesterday I wanted to download some music. I (**b**) *could / couldn't / managed to / didn't manage to* find the correct website but (**c**) *could / couldn't / managed to / didn't manage to* put it onto my MP3 player. My eight-year-old daughter was watching, amused. Later she asked 'Did you manage to put your music onto your MP3 player, dad?' 'Yes,' I said. 'I (**d**) *could / couldn't / managed to / didn't manage to* do it perfectly well, thank you.'

I read the manual again but I still (**e**) *could / couldn't / managed to / didn't manage to* understand anything. In the end I had to ask her to help. She did it in a minute. But then she (**f**) *could / couldn't / managed to / didn't manage to* use a computer at 5 and she (**g**) *could / couldn't / managed to / didn't manage to* record programmes on TV at 6. As for the Internet, she (**h**) *could / couldn't / managed to / didn't manage to* use it for homework ages ago.

It's amazing, isn't it? But she (**i**) *could / couldn't / managed to / didn't manage to* learn the arithmetic times tables until yesterday. Hey, what's 8 times 6?

Modal verbs: probability modals

I You He She It We You They	can can't may might will won't	come this evening. play in the football team. pass the exam.

Use the modals **will, might, could, may** & **won't** to talk about how probable the future is.

I'**ll** see you tomorrow. (= I am 100% certain)

I **won't** see you tomorrow. (= I am 100% certain that I won't)

I **might** see you tomorrow. (= I am 50% certain)

I **could / may** see you tomorrow. (= I am 40% certain)

1 Read the sentences and answer the questions.

a I think Terry will win the race.   most probable
b Charles might win the race.
c Jack could win the race.
d Murray may win the race.
e Bob won't win the race.   least probable

1 Which sentence talks about a prediction that you think will definitely happen? ....

2 Which sentence talks about a prediction that you think certainly won't happen? ....

3 Which sentences talk about something that is possible, but less likely to happen? ....

2 Who will arrive home first?

Complete these sentences with one of these verb forms.

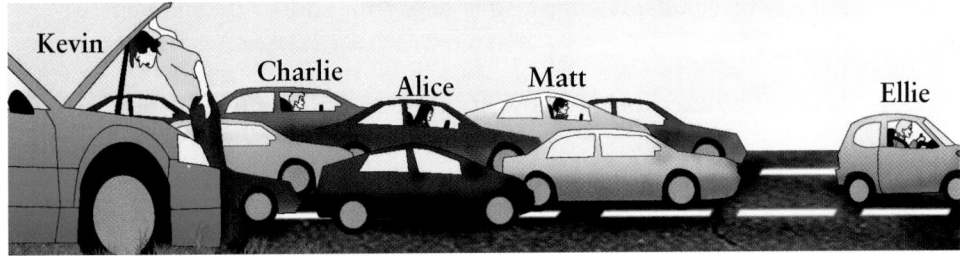

a I think Ellie ....

b Matt ....

c Charlie ....

d Alice ....

e Kevin ....

will	might	may	could	won't

3 Look at these pictures. Write three sentences about what you think the pictures *could*, *might* or *may* be.

a _This could be a plate._

b ....

c ....

d ....

4 Circle the correct word to complete the sentences.

a Oh, you *can't / must* be Kerry's brother. You look almost identical!

b 'Dog Runs from Glasgow to London in five hours.' That *can't / could* be possible. It takes longer to drive that distance by car!

c Tomorrow *may / can't* be sunny or cloudy. It's impossible to say for sure at the moment.

d I *can't / may* go to the party on Friday. I haven't decided yet.

e It *might / can't* be possible to get a ticket for the show at the door, but you usually need to book in advance.

f Francis! *Could / May* it really be you? I haven't heard from you in years!

Verb patterns: *-ing* verbs / *to* + infinitive

I You We They	hate like	listening. playing football.
He She It	loves	taking exercise. watching TV.

When we use two verbs together the second verb is often **verb + -ing**.

 I **love** play**ing** football.
 I **hate** listen**ing** to music.

With some verbs the second verb is **always** -ing.

 I don't **enjoy** watch**ing** TV.
 I **dislike** eat**ing** bananas.

Spacehopper (1970)

Rubik's cube (1980s)

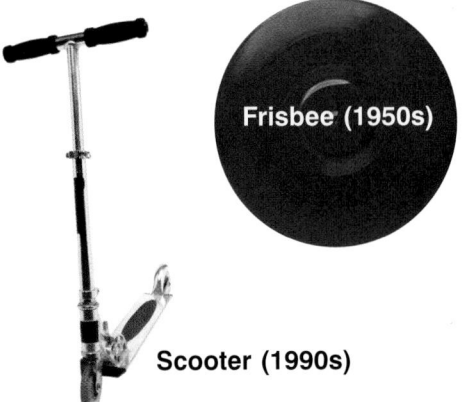

Frisbee (1950s)

Scooter (1990s)

1 Match the toys with the people.

Toys were us

Mary

'I got my first .... for my 6th birthday in 1972. It was a great big ball, filled with air. I bounced around on it all day. My older brother was horrible! He put a little pin through it. Of course the air kept coming out very slowly so one day the ball didn't bounce anymore and my legs touched the floor. He told me that I was too big and fat for it!'

Clive

'I had to spend months in hospital. I lay there doing nothing for days. I hated being there. Then one day the nurse brought me one of those cubes to keep me busy. It was really, really difficult but I did it in the end – and then I changed it all and started playing with it all over again! I wasn't the only one – people bought more than 100 million of them. Yes, the .... was definitely my favourite toy.'

Pete

'My parents couldn't afford to buy us expensive toys. One day, dad came home with a present. Imagine the excitement! But we were really disappointed. It was just a round plastic disc. But that simple disc gave us hours of pleasure. We loved playing with it in the open air. The .... has got to be the most popular toy ever! They have sold more than 200 million in the past 40 years!'

Sally

'My most memorable toy was my .... When I was about 12 those things were really cool. Even older people travelled around the city on them. My sister and I practised pushing with one foot every day. We wanted to go as fast as possible. One day we tried going downhill together on the same one and we had a bad fall. Only little children use them now.'

2 Find the following verbs in the text in exercise 1. Do the activities that follow.

| afford   start   hate   keep   love   practise   try   want |

3 Complete the chart with verbs followed by another verb ending in *-ing* (e.g. *I enjoy doing*), or by another verb with *to* + infinitive (e.g. *I can't afford to do*).

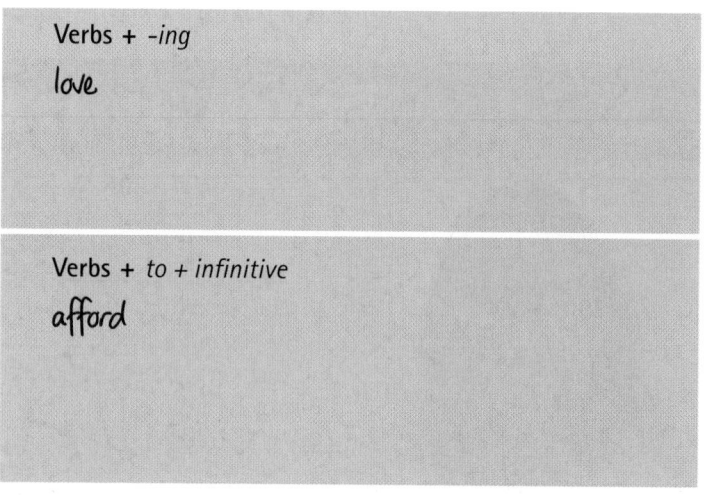

Verbs + *-ing*

love

Verbs + *to* + infinitive

afford

4 Complete these sentences about yourself. Use a verb ending in *-ing* or a verb with *to* + infinitive.

a I enjoy .... at home.

b I love .... with my friends.

c I often practise .... in my English class.

d I hate .... at the weekend.

e I can afford .... , but I can't afford ....

f My best friend wants ....

g My parents keep ....

h I always try .... other people.

i I have decided .... as soon as I can.

5 Read the text. Underline the correct verbs. Be careful, sometimes both verbs are possible.

Tango Mad

When my friend invited me (**a**) *to see / seeing* an Argentinean tango show, I wasn't keen. But I wasn't disappointed. The dance is elegant and romantic. I like to (**b**) *try / trying* new things, so I decided (**c**) *to learn / learning*.

I can't afford (**d**) *to go / going* to Argentina so I started (**e**) *to take / taking* a weekly class in a local college. But once is not enough – now I try (**f**) *to go / going* at least twice a week. I'm tango mad!

It isn't an easy dance to learn (and I hate (**g**) *to wear / wearing* those high heels!), and you really have to be fit. But I want (**h**) *to be / being* like the women in the show, so I keep (**i**) *to practise / practising*.

Sometimes, when I'm alone in the house, I put on my tango clothes (and heels!) and I practise (**j**) *to do / doing* the new steps in front of a video. I try (**k**) *to copy / copying* the people on the screen. But really, it takes two to tango!

6 Complete the sentences with the correct form of the verbs in brackets.

a No, thank you. I really dislike ......*dancing*...... (dance).

b Don't forget .... (revise) your vocabulary!

c Mark promised .... (help) Cecilia with her project.

d Did you finish .... (write) the invitations?

e Imagine .... (go) to Argentina to learn the tango!

f Stop .... (talk) so loudly, please. I can't hear the film.

g I asked him to stop, but he continued .... (talk).

h Yes, please! I love .... (go) on picnics.

7 What do you say in these situations? Write sentences using verbs from exercise 6.

a You're having a party. Your friend said 'I can help with the cooking'. Now he's watching the football.

Don't forget to help with the cooking!

b Your friend was writing a report. You are not sure she has finished. What do you ask your friend?

....

....

....

c You're in a concert. The person behind you is talking on a mobile phone.

....

....

....

d Your friend has a grammar test tomorrow. What do you tell your friend?

....

....

....

e Someone invites you to see a horror movie. You strongly dislike horror movies.

....

....

....

Verb patterns: verbs with two objects

		Indirect object	Direct object
She	lent	me	a present.
I	gave	him	some money.

When we use to **objects** we often put the **indirect** object first (1) and the **direct** object second (2).

> He gave **me** (1) **a present** (2).
> I lent **him** (1) **some money** (2).

		Direct object		Indirect object
I	gave	a present	to	my friend.
She	lent	a coat		her mother.

Use a **preposition** with the **indirect** object if the **direct** object is first.

> I gave a present (2) **to** my friend (1).
> She lent her coat (2) **to** her mother (1).

		Direct object		Indirect object
I	gave	it	to	my friend.
She	lent	a coat		her mother.

Use the **direct** object first if both objects are **pronouns**.

> Give **it** (2) **to me** (1)!
> I'm going to lend **it** (2) **to you** (1).

1 Read these sentences. Which are correct? Which are wrong? Put a tick or a cross in the boxes. If necessary, write correct sentences in the spaces provided.

a She gave a present to me. ☐

....

b She gave a present to my mother. ☐

....

c She gave it me. ☐

....

d She gave me it. ☐

....

e She gave to me a present. ☐

....

f She gave my mother a present. ☐

....

g She gave to my mother a present. ☐

....

2 Put the following words in order to make correct sentences.

a a / letter / me / She / wrote

....

b bought / for / him / I / it

....

c a / for / girlfriend / He / his / played / song

....

d a / birthday / for / gave / me / mother / My / my / radio

....

e a / cost / It / lot / money / of / them

....

f a / good / He / offered / price / them

....

g a / father / I / lot / money / my / of / owe / to

....

3 Who did what? Complete the story using the verbs in the box.
   Use the past tense if possible.

Steve (a) .... Jim some money and Jim (b) .... an expensive present for Judy – a beautiful jacket. Judy was very happy and (c) .... the present to her friend Ingrid. Two weeks passed. Steve wasn't very happy. He (d) .... Jim an email. You (e) .... me some money, he said. Jim (f) .... him a text message. '2 bad. U can 4get it,' he texted. Steve (g) .... the text message to his friend Philip, so Philip rang up Jim and (h) .... him a message. '(i) .... Steve his money,' he said, but Jim said 'no'. 'Right,' said Steve, 'I'm going to (j) .... him a lesson' but then Jim rang him up. 'I'll (k) .... you half today,' he said, 'and half next week. Is that OK?' And it was. But Steve isn't going to lend Jim any money ever again!

| buy give leave lend |
| owe pay read send |
| show teach write |

4 Write the following sentences with *borrow* and *lend*.

a When you .... money, you give money to someone (and you expect it back).
b When you .... money, you take money from someone and you expect to give it back.

5 Read this paragraph and answer the questions below using complete sentences.

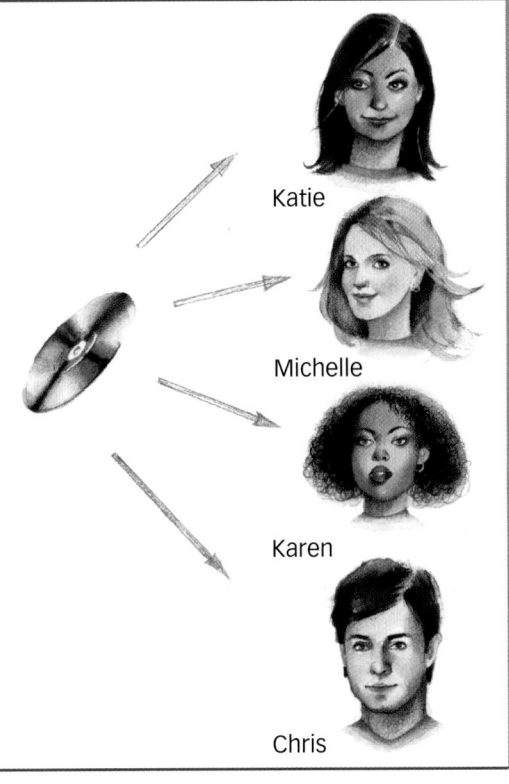

Katie
Michelle
Karen
Chris

Katie bought <u>a new CD</u>. She listened to it twice and then Michelle borrowed it. Michelle was showing it to Chris and she left it at his house. The next day, Chris asked Michelle if he could borrow it, because he liked it. After a week Katie asked Michelle to give the CD back to her. Michelle said, "I'm sorry, Katie, but I lent it to Chris." So Katie phoned Chris. "Yes, I borrowed it from Michelle," said Chris, "but then I bought the CD at the music shop." 'So, who has my CD?" said Katie. "I gave it back to Michelle and then she lent it to Karen."

a What did Katie buy?
   a new CD
b How many times did she listen to it? ....
c Who did Katie lend it to?
   ....
d Whose house did Michelle leave it at? ....
e Who asked to borrow the CD?
   ....
f Who did he ask? ....
g When did Katie ask Michelle for the CD? ....
h What did Chris buy?
   ....
i Who did he give the CD to?
   ....
j Who borrowed the CD from Michelle? ....

6 Now underline the direct objects in the text, and circle the indirect objects.

Verb patterns: verb + object + (to) + infinitive

I She We	asked begged ordered	him them you	(not) to	leave. stay. talk.

Use <u>Verb</u> + **object** + **to** + **infinitive** with verbs like *ask, beg, order, want & warn*.
He <u>asked</u> me **to show** my passport.
They <u>warned</u> me not **to try** and escape.

I She We	let made	him them you	leave. stay. talk.

Don't use **to** with a few verbs like *let & make*.
She **let** me **finish** the exam paper.
He **made** me **wait** for hours.

1 Mary is 16 and trains every week to be a boxer. She wants to enter a competition. Report what people said using the verbs in the box.

ask	beg	invite	order
remind	~~tell~~	want	warn

a Frank (Mary's trainer): You must enter the competition.

Frank told her to enter the competition

b Martin (boyfriend): Don't enter the competition. Please, please, please, please don't!

....

c Paul (brother): I'd like my sister to enter the competition.

....

d Sam Gordon (competition organiser): Would you like to enter my competition? Please do.

....

e Mr Graham (father): Enter the competition. I'm telling you.

....

f Sue (her sister): Don't forget to enter the competition!

....

g Brad (her close friend): Don't enter the competition! It's a bad idea. Very dangerous. Stay away.

....

h Anita (best friend): Please enter the competition. Then I would be happy.

....

2 Circle the correct form to complete these sentences.

a She let her son (play) / to play in the sea.

b Maria warned him *not to fall* / *to not fall* in the river.

c Cristina told Jason *not to stay* / *not stay* very late.

d Laura and Frank invited them *to come* / *come to* to dinner.

e Katie taught her son *to cook* / *cook*.

f We begged them *not to wait* / *not wait* too long.

g She wanted *to go* / *go* to the party.

3 Use an appropriate verb from exercise 2 to write what they said.

a 'Don't forget to take your books,' Mary to Jake.

   Mary reminded Jake to take his books.

b 'Would you like to come to dinner?' Ron and Jody to Kevin.

c 'You have to go home now,' Susie to Michelle and Claire.

d 'Do you want to watch TV?' Chris to Mike.

e 'Put it down now!' David to Janie.

f 'That's dangerous. Don't go in there,' Emma to Richie and Charles.

g 'I'd like some cake,' Ellie.

h 'Please, please help me,' Alice to Marty.

4 Use the verbs in the box to rewrite these sentences.

| ask   remind   reassure   suggest |
| promise   order   beg |

a Mother angrily to child: Go to bed at once!

....

b One girl to another girl: I think you should wear the blue one.

....

c Customer to shop assistant: May I have my money back?

....

d Driver to traffic warden: Please don't give me a parking ticket.

....

e Boy looking romantically at girl: I will never, ever leave you.

....

f Nurse to patient in hospital: Don't worry. You'll be fine.

....

g Mother to daughter: 'Don't forget, it's Dad's birthday in two days.'

....

5 Complete the conversation with *make* or *let*.

MUM: I can't (a) .... you go out late at night, Janice. You're only 17.

JANICE: Oh, Mum! You can't (b) .... me stay at home every night! You'll
(c) .... me lose all my friends!

MUM: Well, do their mothers (d) .... them to go out at night?

JANICE: Not on their own, but they (e) .... them go out in groups or pairs!

MUM: OK, I'll (f) .... you to go out as long as you have a friend with you. Will that
(g) .... you happy?

JANICE: Oh, yes! Thanks, Mum.

Review unit A

1 Match each sentence with the explanation of its meaning.

Explanations

a a repeated action or habit in the present
b a prediction about the future
c an interrupted action in the past
d something that was in progress in the past
e a completed past action
f connects the present and the past
g a general fact which is true
h an unplanned decision
i something in progress at the moment
j describes what happens in a film, book, programme or story
k a plan
l a habit in the past

Sentences

1 Any plans for tomorrow?
   Yes, I'm going to do some housework at last.
2 It gets darker at night.
3 Have you seen this movie yet? It's wonderful.
4 We were watching TV last night when my aunt called from Australia.
5 The show is about a woman who lives in France.
6 We used to go to the movies once a week. Now it's impossible.
7 You have to see that play. You'll love it!
8 Every day he eats lunch at Harry's restaurant.
9 I'm taking dance classes at the moment.
10 The sun was shining as she walked through the park.
11 You say the number and I'll write it down.
12 He passed the test.

a ....
b ....
c ....
d ....
e ....
f ....
g ....
h ....
i ....
j ....
k ....
l ....

2 Complete these dialogues with the correct tense.

JAMES: Where (**a**) ...*does*............ he ...*live*............... (live) now?

MARIE: He (**b**) .... (live) in a strange little house in the mountains.

MARTIN: (**c**) .... you ever .... (be) to Egypt?

JOANNE: No, I (**d**) .... , but I'm (**e**) .... (go) to Cairo next year.

MUM: What time (**f**) .... your train .... (leave) yesterday?

BOBBY: It (**g**) .... (leave) at 9.00 and (**h**) .... (arrive) at 11.30.

OLD MAN: I can't open this door. (**i**) .... you .... (help) me?

YOUNG WOMAN: Of course! I (**j**) .... (open) it for you.

3 Complete this paragraph with appropriate verb forms.

Stephen Hawking, the world famous physicist,
(**a**) ....*has been*............ (be) worried for a long time about
computers. He (**b**) .... (be) worried,
because computers (**c**) .... (develop) very
quickly. He (**d**) .... (think) that in the
future, computers (**e**) .... (become) more
intelligent than humans. He (**f**) ....
(believe) that computers with artificial intelligence could
control the world.

Critic's choice

4 Complete these sentences with a suitable word from the box.

a Mum, will you ....*buy*........... me a new toy, please?

b Did you .... the money you
.... to your sister?

c This is a letter to the manager.
I'm .... it to him to complain
about the hotel room.

d Will you .... me that book when
you have .... it?

e I'd like to .... your car, if you don't mind.

f Come here and I'll .... you how to use this new
computer program.

g Do you think you could .... me how to play the piano?

h He didn't want to .... his children alone with the new babysitter,
because she seemed strange.

~~buy~~	borrow
leave	lend
owe	pay
read	send
show	teach

5 Complete the sentences with *can*, *can't*, *could* or *couldn't*.

a She's a famous singer. She .... sing very well. But .... you believe that she
.... sing at all when she was younger? It's true! She was so shy, she .... even stand
up and read in front of her classmates!

b 'I'm afraid you have a broken ankle,' the doctor said. 'You .... leave hospital today, but you
.... walk on this leg for a while. You certainly .... do any sports.'

c When I heard him say that, I .... believe my ears. I .... help my team to win the
cup in the match on Saturday! I felt really miserable.

d 'Cheer up!' said the doctor. 'You .... still do a lot of things. You .... listen to music,
you .... watch TV ... and you .... watch your team play!'

Review unit B

1 Circle the correct answer.

a Paris is .... city in France.

/ *the largest* / *the larger* / *largest*

b I don't want .... sugar, thank you.

/ *some* / *any* / *many*

c I'd like .... boiled potatoes, please.

/ *some* / *one* / *much*

d How .... apple juice do you need?

/ *many* / *any* / *much*

e I just need .... apples for this apple pie.

/ *few* / *little* / *a few*

f Nicole Kidman is .... than Julia Roberts.

/ *popular* / *most popular* / *more popular*

g Who is the .... singer in the world?

/ *better* / *good* / *best*

h Iron is .... than feathers.

/ *heavier* / *more heavy* / *heaviest*

i The building on the left is .... than the other one.

/ *more high* / *higher* / *highest*

j This is .... book I've ever read.

/ *the more interesting* / *most interesting* / *the most interesting*

k Do you like .... animals?

/ *the* / *a* / *–*

l I'm hungry. I'd like .... sandwich, please.

/ *the* / *a* / *–*

m I enjoyed walking .... the town yesterday.

/ *through* / *below* / *over*

n I was driving .... a street near my house, looking at the flowers, when I saw a strange animal.

/ *into* / *along* / *inside*

2 Read these sentences and write whether they refer to the past, the present or the future.

a This house was built in 1965.

..past..........

b Next week we're visiting my grandmother in France. ....

c I'm working on a grammar exercise at the moment. ....

d My mother has lived in Russia for twenty years. ....

e My car is being washed at the moment.

....

f Did you watch that TV programme last night? ....

g Will you help me with my homework?

....

h We live by the sea. ....

i Last night at nine o'clock I was watching TV. ....

3 Name the tense used in each sentence in exercise 2.

a ..simple past (passive)................

b ....

c ....

d ....

e ....

f ....

g ....

h ....

i ....

4   Complete the text with the best word, 1 - 3 below.

Two women were walking
(**a**) ....through.... a local cemetery
filming with a video camera.
Suddenly (**b**) .... camera
stopped working. They kept
recording with (**c**) ....
portable tape recorder that one
woman had (**d**) .... her
pocket. They chatted about the
beauty of the cemetery as they
walked (**e**) .... the path.
Later when they listened to
(**f**) .... recording, they heard
something very strange. After one
of (**g**) .... women said "What
(**h**) .... peaceful area," a
creepy whisper said "peaceful."
They played (**i**) .... tape
about 20 times and heard the
voice each time.

a	1) over	2) below	③ through
b	1) one	2) the	3) a
c	1) a	2) the	3) a
d	1) in	2) to	3) of
e	1) into	2) along	3) inside
f	1) ----	2) a	3) the
g	1) the	2) a	3) one
h	1) one	2) a	3) ----
i	1) a	2) the	3) ----

ANSWER KEY

Unit 1

1 1 syllable – fast, high, large, tall, small
  2 syllables – sunny, friendly
  3 syllables – beautiful, popular
2 a more b smaller c more d fewer e greater
  f larger g smaller h lower I higher j longer
3 a more interesting than, more easily
  b better than, more cheaply
  c faster, smaller
  d more comfortable than, more quickly
  e lower than, colder
4 a Stadium Australia is larger than the Millennium Stadium.
  b Edmonton Stadium is smaller than Stadium Australia.
  c Kingda Ka is taller than Top Thrill Dragster.
  d In Australia Horse Racing is more populat than Rugby League.
  e Pipeline Bungee is higher than Mokai Canyon.
  f In Britain, football is more popular than cricket.
  g The Millennium Stadium is bigger than Edmonton Stadium.
  h In the USA, American football is more popular than basketball.
5 a Kingda Ka
  b Yes
  c Basketball
  d Smaller
  e South Africa
  f Australia

Unit 2

1 a worst
  b most boring
  c cheapest
  d most cramped
  e deepest
  f most expensive
  g fastest
  h fattest
  i funniest
  j best
  k highest
  l most interesting
  m longest
  n narrowest
  o most spacious
  p thinnest
  q ugliest
  r most uncomfortable
2 a the worst
  b the most interesting
  c the largest
  d the most uncomfortable

e the cheapest
f the most expensive
g the funniest
h the best
i the narrowest
j the thinnest
3 a Flat B is the smallest.
  b Flat C is the sunniest.
  c Flat C is the largest.
  d Flat B is the nearest to town.
  e Flat A is the most modern.
  f Flat B is the noisiest.
  g Flat A is the most expensive.
4 a Flat C is the largest.
  b Flat B is the darkest.
  c Flat B is the smallest.
  d Flat C is the furthest from town.
  e Flat B is the least modern / most old-fashioned.
  f Flat C is the quietest.
  g Flat B is the cheapest.
5 a The longest river is the Nile.
  b The tallest telecommunications tower is the CN Tower.
  c The largest country is Russia.
  d The highest waterfalls are the Angel Falls.
  e The deepest caves are in Lamprechtshofen, Austria.
  f The most crowded city is Hong Kong.
6 a oldest
  b longest
  c furthest
  d smallest
  e most expensive

Unit 3

1 a bored
  b boring
  c interested
  d interesting
  e disappointing
  f disappointed
2 a relaxing
  b interesting
  c interested
  d tired
  e tiring
  g relaxed
  g worried
  h amusing
  i amusing
3 1 Picture b   2 Picture a
4 a excited b surprising c shocking d interesting
  e boring f tired g relaxing h disappointing
5 a frightening b worried c boring d surprising
  e amusing f interested

Unit 4

1 1 a 2 c 3 b 4 c 5 a 6 b
2 a The b The c a d The e a f - g a h the
   i the j the k an
3 1 b 2 f 3 h 4 a 5 g 6 d 7 e 8 c
4 a –, –
   b an, the
   c –, the
   d The, an
   e A, a, The, –
   f the
   g the
   h The, –
   i The, –, –, the
5 1 a b 2 c e 5 e 6 f 5 g 4 h 1 i 6

Unit 5

1 a 4 b 6 c 1 d 8 e 3 f 7 g 2 h 5
2 a are not lying down/don't lie down: won't be able to
   b will get: rest
   c study: will pass
   d will feel: drink
   e won't get: don't exercise
   f eat: will ... get
   g catch: go out
   h help: wash
   i listen to: will hurt
   j go: doesn't finish
4 a like, will love
   b will have, use
   c will stay, wash
   d is, will enjoy
   e won't be, change
   f don't have, will fill, (will) save
5 1 c 2 b 3 d 4 a 5 f 6 e
6 *Suggested answers*
   1 If you like exciting books, you'll like this one/book.
   2 Buy these shoes if you like style and elegance.
   3 If you use this shampoo, your hair will shine.
   4 You'll love this drink if you like coffee.

Unit 6

1 1 b 2 a
2 a P b T c T d P e T f P g P
3 a 3 b 4 c 1 d 6 e 2 f 5
5 a 1 b 2 c 3 d 2

Unit 7

1 Countable: problem, crisp
   Uncountable: meat, sugar, stress, crisps
   Countable and uncountable: fruit/fruits, oranges, fish
   salad/salads, chocolate/chocolates, apples, bananas
2 Countable: things, body, movement, shoes, mind,
   person
   Uncountable: stress, energy, equipment, clothes, people
   Countable and uncountable: exercise (exercises)
3 sugar [U]
   oil [U]
   cakes [C]

cookies [C]
potatoes [C]
meat [U]
chicken [U]
fish [U]
rice [U]
pasta [U]
yoghurt [U]
vegetables [C]
fruit [U]
juice [U
4 a a shoe b an exercise c a chicken d stress
   e clothes f equipment g an orange h furniture
   i fish
5 a NP b NP c papers d NP e NP f NP g NP
   h apples i NP
6 salad, soup, coffee, cake, fruit, chocolate

Unit 8

1 a little = 30 grams of butter, a few = four tomatoes,
   lots of = 24 eggs, a lot of = a kilo of cheese,
   no = millilitres of milk,
   no = 0 potatoes
2 **Large quantities:**
   Countable nouns: lots of, a lot of
   Uncountable nouns: lots of, a lot of
   Small quantities:
   Countable nouns: a few
   Uncountable nouns: a little
   No quantity:
   Countable nouns: no, not any
   Uncountable nouns: no, not any
3 a any b some/many c A lot of, Many, Lots of
   d no, no e A few f Few g any h any
4 a a few / some
   b some
   c some, much
   d some
   e Some
   f some, a few
6 a much, lots of
   b many, a few
   c much, no
   d any, any
   e a few, any

Unit 9

1 a books – collect, read
   b films – watch, go to
   c football – watch, go to, play
   d horses – ride
   e music – listen to, play, read
   f shopping – go
   g stamps – collect
   h bird watching - go, go to
2 a cycling b swimming
   c pistol shooting d fencing
   e running f bowling g show jumping
   h life-saving i weightlifting
   Life-saving and bowling are not Olympic sports.

3 a pistol shooting b swimming
   c running d show-jumping
   e fencing
4 a playing
   b watching
   c riding
   d reading
   e collecting
   f like going
   g listening to
5 a watching
   b shopping
   c Smoking
   d Swimming
   e buying
   f boxing

Unit 10

1 a between b in c next to d opposite
   e behind f inside g above, below h outside
   i in front of j on top of k under
3 a Jack's at Steve's house, b Lucy's in a (Turkish) café,
   c Di is in/at the station, d Judy is at a bus stop,
   e Roger is at home, f Pat's at the hospital,
   g Jim's in (the) hospital, h Vince is at the station,
   i John is at/in the cinema, j Hazel is at work.
4 a under b between c above d on top of e next to
   f behind
5 a the cupboard
   b The mirror
   c the door / the room
   d a cat
   e the picture
   f the desk

Unit 11

1 The correct sequence is 1 h, 2 d, 3 i, 4 f, 5 g, 6 k, 7 e,
   8 a, 9 c, 10 j, 11 b, 12 l
2 see map
3 route needs to be drawn on above map
   Walk along the road until you get to the bridge.
   Walk over the bridge and then turn left. Go down
   the hill towards the park. Go into the park and
   walk towards the lake. Turn left at the lake and
   walk towards the street. Turn left and walk down
   the street. Turn right onto Green Street and Katie's
   house is the first house on the right.

Unit 12

1 a goes, watches, goes, doesn't eat
   b play, answer, win
   c buy, watch
   d do, like
   e marries
2 a cries b buys c watches d read e doesn't have
   f have g doesn't have, record
3 a does, want
   b does, do
   c Why, eat
   d Why do

e When do, watch
f Do, like
4 a interview b read c watch d means
   e gets up f doesn't get up g arrive h meet
   i interview j prepare k do (they) enjoy l goes
   m tries n see o doesn't have
5 a
Natasha gets up at 3.15.
Dermot doesn't get up so early.
They both arrive at the studios at 4.30.
She goes to bed at 8.
They meet with the producer of the programme.
Natasha and Dermot usually interview 12 people a day
and they prepare carefully.
   b
Millions of viewers watch it every day.
The working hours are terrible.
   c
The presenters interview people and read the news.
6 a What is your job? / What do you do for a living?
   b What time is the programme? / What time does the
      programme start and finish?
   c What time do you get up?
   d Does Dermot get up at 3.15 too?
   e When do you see your friends?
   f Do you like your job?
7 a Do you have time for breakfast?
   b How many days a week do you work?
   c What does your family think about your working
      hours?
   d Do you buy lots of new clothes for work?

Unit 13

1 1 a Kenny loves Lola. 1 b Sally loves Kenny.
   2 a Kenny admires Bart Simpson. 2 b Kenny's little
      brother admires Kenny.
   3 a Kenny dislikes 'goody-goody' people. 3 b 'Goody-
      goody' people (probably) dislike Kenny.
2 Asking about the object: Who does Kenny admire?
   Who does Kenny love?
   What kind of people does Kenny dislike?
   What kind of people probably dislike Kenny?
   Asking about the subject:
   Who admires Kenny? Who loves Kenny?
3 a Who wants to be a millionaire? Everybody does.
   b What does everybody want to be? A millionaire.
   c What do many people read? Magazines about
      celebrities.
   d Who reads magazines about celebrities? Many
      people do.
   e Who doesn't like photographers? Celebrities.
   f What don't celebrities like? Photographers.
   g What do monkeys eat? Nuts and fruits.
   h Who eats nuts and fruits? Monkeys do.
4 a Nancy b Norah c Nancy, Norah
   d Nancy, Norah e Nancy, Norah
   f Norah and/or Nancy
5 a does Nancy like b likes c loves
   d does Barry love e does Nancy watch
   f admires g admires h does Norah read
   i watches

Unit 14

1 a are playing (on Sunday) F, 'we're training' (at this moment) P
   b 'I'm meeting' (tomorrow) F, 'I'm checking' (right now) P
   c 'I'm practising' P, 'I'm taking' (tomorrow) F
   d 'I'm working' P, 'we're having' (on Saturday) F
2 Time expressions are usually used with F meanings.
3 Present: now, today, at this moment, at 8 o'clock, this week
   Future: today, tomorrow, at 8 o'clock, next week, on 25th May, on Tuesday, this week, in the summer, Monday afternoon
4 a R/H b T c T d R/H
5 a wants b knows c is training d is working
   e is not doing f washes g prepares
   h does (he) feel i am writing j am (just) working
   k (I am) learning
6 a What do you know about a chef's job?
   b What do you want to be?
   c What are you doing/studying
   d Where are you working
   e What do you do (all day)?
   f Why are you writing down your mum's secrets?
   g Are you writing a book?

Unit 15

1 a will go
   b Will, be
      will be
   c will ring / phone / call
   d will like
      will love
2 a: b and d
   b: a and c
3 a P b P c UD d P e P f UD g P h UD i UD
4 a will be b will be c won't go d won't go
   e 'll take f 'll make g Will ... make h will be
   i won't pass j 'll do k will ... be l 'll be
   m 'll have to n 'll pass
5 a 3 b 1 c 4 d 2
   Predictions: a, c
   Unplanned decisions: b, d
6 a will win
   b will get
   c will/'ll come
   d won't be
   e will beat
   f Will (the race) be
   g will be
   h won't be able
   i will (probably) have to
   j will/'ll record

Unit 16

1 a past b future c present d future e past/present
   f present g future
2 a are you going to do
   b I'm going to go
   c is going to get

d are going to have
   e Are you going to take
   f I'm not going to take
   g are you going to do
   h I'm not going to do
3 a They're going to have breakfast.
   b He's going to go swimming.
   c They're going to get married.
   d They're going to go to Australia.
4 a False. They're going to get wet.
   b False. He's not going to fail the mathematics exam. / He's going to pass the mathematics exam.
   c False. They're going to go skiing.
   d True
   e False. They're going to do their English homework.
   f True

Unit 17

1 **Conversation 1:**
   a are you going to b 'll c Are ... going to d 'm going to e are going to f 'll
   Conversation 2:
   g 'll h 'll i 'm going to j Will k won't
2 a planned intention b prediction c planned intention
   d planned intention e planned intention f prediction
   g prediction h prediction i planned intention
   j prediction k prediction
3 *Suggested answers:*
   On Monday she's going to go to work early.
   On Tuesday she's going to have a meeting.
   She's going to have lunch with her mother on Wednesday.
   On Thursday she's going to go to the gym in the evening.
   She's going to work late on Friday.
4 a I'm going to study
   b I'll probably
   c I'll carry
   d are you going to, We're going to
   e I'll
   f I'm going to get some painters to do it., I'll help you
5 a 5 b 3 c 2 d 8 e 7 f 4 g 6 h 1
6 a going to
   b 'm going to
   c 'll
   d will
   e 'm not going to, 'm going to
   f are, going to
   g 're going to
   h 'll
   i Are, going to
   j 'll
   k 'm going to
   l won't

Unit 18

1 a P b P c F d P e P f F g F
2 *Suggested answers*
   a We're watching a DVD now. (present) We're watching a DVD tonight. (future)

b I'm taking an English lesson right now. (present) I'm taking an English lesson next week. (future)

c We're doing some grammar exercises at the moment. (present) We're doing some grammar exercises from Monday. (future)

d He's working on a new project at present. (present) He's working on a new project from Monday. (future)

e Are you working right now? (present) Are you working later tonight? (future)

4 a What is he going to do
He's going to meet Elena. / He's meeting Elena.

b What is he going to do / doing
he's going shopping
he's going to go to the cinema

c What is he going to do / What is he doing
he's going to walk Billie's dog. Then, he's going to watch tennis.

d What is he doing / is he going to do
He's playing badminton / going to play badminton, and he's going out with Chris.

e What is he going to do / doing
He's going to the bank, then he's going to have lunch with Tania.

f What is he going to do / doing
He's going to go swimming, he's going to Rob's party

Unit19

1 1 e 2 g 3 f 4 d 5 h 6 b 7 a 8 c

2 **Conversation 1:**
a Have, eaten
b tried
c Did, like
d was

Conversation 2:
a saw
b Have, seen
c haven't been
d went
e did, see
f was

3 a has gone, left
b didn't recognise, Have, lost
c 've been
d have forgotten
e gave up, have forgotten
f opened, haven't been
g improved, has got
h failed, felt, have just spoken

4 a Have you heard the news? The Prime Minister has resigned.
b Long ago the Egyptians used hieroglyphics for communication.
c I haven't seen you for ages. Have you been away?
d I've just come back from Italy.
e Alexander Graham Bell invented the telephone.
f Have you finished reading that book yet?
g Yes, I lent it to Gavin yesterday.

Unit 20

1 a since 1991/for XX years
b since 2004/for X years
c since (month)/ for three months
d since 2004/for X years
e since he was 12/since 1992/for XX years
f since (choose a month)/for X months
g since he was 18/since 1998/for X years
h since 2005/for X years

2 a for
b since
c for
d since
e since
g since
h since

3 a for b since c for d since f for g since g for
h for i since j since

4 a for five years
b for three months
c since 2000
d since she was a child
e for a long time

Unit 21

1 a laugh b memorise c repeat d want e forget f find
g feel h give i have j meet k put l try m write

2 a met b gave c write d memorised e repeated
f wanted/tried g found h forgot i had j felt k put

3 a happened, did (you) meet, were, was
b did (you) learn
c did (the event) happen, did (the people) do
d did (you last) use, did (you) phone, was

4 a did not live b was c moved d lived e had
f started g studied h graduated i did not like
j was k married l used m died

5 a (Where) did the Freud family move to (in 1860?)
b (When) did Freud move to Vienna?
c (Where) did he/Freud (go to school?)
d (When) did he/Freud move to England?
e (How many) brothers and sisters did he/Freud have?
f (Who) did he/Freud marry?
g (When) did he/Freud die?

Unit 22

1 a were doing b were working c was having
d working e was having f was looking up

2 a weren't working b weren't doing c rang
d were talking e was helping f arrived
g hung up h heard i wrote

3 a heard, got
b saw, was having
c was having, was working
d were talking, rang
e did (Laura) do, arrived
f got, heard
g were not talking, did not enjoy

4 a I hurt my shoulder.
b were holding hands
c was going to the hairdresser's.

d was having dinner.

e was sending a text message.

f was wearing some new boots.

g was buying tickets for the show.

h were dancing.

5 **a** wasn't raining **b** was sitting **c** was babysitting

d was watching **e** were talking **f** were laughing

g was screaming **h** was trying **i** was trying

j was parking

Unit 23

1 **c** A gorilla escaped from a van.

2 **a** A window cleaner was cleaning a shop window.

b A man (with a cap) was walking his dog.

c A group of children was walking to school.

d Three people were waiting for the bus.

e A boy was delivering newspapers on his bike.

f A man was reading a newspaper on the corner.

g A woman was bringing in the milk.

h Two girls were jogging.

i The baker was standing outside his bakery.

j Some people were having breakfast in a café.

3 **a** What was the window cleaner doing?

b What were you doing at 7 o'clock yesterday morning?

c Where was the man standing?

d What were the people waiting for?

e Where were the children going?

f What was everybody looking at?

g Why was the gorilla walking in the street?

4 **a** F He wasn't reading a book, he was reading a newspaper.

b F

c F She wasn't bringing in the newspaper, she was bringing in the milk.*

* (Background note: In Britain, milk is delivered by the milkman, to your doorstep.)

d F They weren't riding their bikes to school, they were walking to school.

e T

f F He wasn't walking a large dog, he was walking a small dog.

g F They weren't wearing jeans, they were wearing school uniforms.

5 **a** was shining **b** was feeling **c** arrived

d was closing **e** got **f** stood **g** offered

h was reading **i** was (only) trying **j** was raining

k wasn't smiling

6 **Pattern 1**

a The train was leaving when I got to the platform.

b The man was closing his ticket window just as I got there.

c She was reading her paper when a child put his hand in her bag.

Pattern 2

d When I left the house the sun was shining and I was feeling happy.

Pattern 3

e I stood all the way while some children sat comfortably.

7 **a** was (Brian) doing, arrived

did (he) do, arrived

b were (you) doing, saw

did (you) do, saw

c were (you) dreaming, rang

did (you) do, rang

d was (your friend) watching, got

did (you) watch, were

8 **a** practises / was practising

b was arriving / arrived

c were ringing / rang

d waited / was waiting

e went / was going

f had / were having

Unit 24

1 about 100 years old

2 **Affirmative:**

There used to be (just one telephone) in our village.

We used to play board games.

We used to watch a film occasionally.

Negative:

Girls didn't use to stay in school for very long.

We didn't use to have a car.

3 **a** used to have

b didn't use to go out often, used to play board games

c used to wear fun clothes, used to have interesting hairstyles, used to love dancing

d didn't use to drive

4 **Past habits:**

a I used to play in a rock band!

b We used to play at parties and clubs.

c I used to miss playing, terribly.

Present habits:

d I usually play my guitar just at family parties.

Completed actions:

e I got married so I left the band.

5 **a** British businessmen used to wear bowler hats until the 1960s.

b Some ancient Romans didn't use to wash their hair very often. They only used to wash it on 13th August, the birthday of the goddess Diana.

c The ancient Egyptians used to paint the picture of their worst enemy inside their sandals.

d In the 1970s punks used to put egg, butter or toothpaste in their hair. Then they used to paint it with food colouring or spray paint.

e In the 19th century women used to wear very tight corsets to look thin. Some women used to faint or break their ribs.

6 **a** What did British businessmen use to wear?

b How often did some ancient Romans use to wash their hair?

c Why did the ancient Egyptians use to paint a picture of their enemy inside their sandals?

d When did some ancient Romans use to wash their hair?

e Why did some women use to faint in the 19th century

Unit 25

1   a Could b Could c can't d Can't e can't
2   Examples for Use 1: d, f
     Examples for Use 2: a, c, e, g
     Examples for Use 3: b
3   a 4 b 3 c 1 d 2
4   a With this software you can design posters, but you
        can't make them in colour.
     b Can you download music from the Internet?
     c Can you help me with this program?
     d Can you take photos with this mobile?
     e Rizwan can take photos of plants.
     f I can fix a computer quickly.
     g Howa can't mix music.
     h Can you take the CD out of the machine?

Unit 26

1   a managed to
     b could, could, couldn't
     c couldn't, managed to
     d managed to, couldn't, couldn't
     e didn't manage to, could
2   a could b could c could, could d could, couldn't
     e managed to f could, managed to
     g managed to, couldn't
3   a 1 b 2 c 2 d 1
4   a couldn't b managed to   c didn't manage to
     d managed to e couldn't f could g could
     h could i didn't manage to
5   a managed to b Could c couldn't
     d didn't manage to e couldn't/didn't manage to
     f could g couldn't h manage to i could

Unit 27

1   Sentence a talks about a 'certain' prediction.
     Sentence e talks about a prediction that you think
     definitely won't happen.
     Sentences b, c, d talk about something that is possible
     but not certain.
2   *Suggested answers*
     a I think Ellie will arrive home first.
     b Matt may / might / could arrive home first.
     c Charlie may / might / could arrive home first.
     d Alice may / might / could arrive home first.
     e Kevin won't arrive home first.
3   *Suggested answers*
     a This could be a plate. This might be a saucer. This
        may be a cup.
        (It is a cup.)
     b This could be a spoon. This might be a spade. This
        may be a door handle.
        (It is a fork.)

     c This could be a computer. This might be a DVD
        player. This may be a TV.
        (It is a TV.)
     d This could be a telephone. This might be a
        calculator. This may be a bank machine.
        (It is a telephone.)
4   a must b can't c may d may e might f Could

Unit 28

1   Mary: space hopper ('a big ball', 'bouncing around')
     Clive: Rubik's cube ('one of those cubes')
     Imran: Frisbee ('round plastic disc', ' ...those discs flew
     from our hands')
     Sally: scooter ('...travelled on them, pushing with one
     foot')
3   Verbs + -ing: hate, keep, like, practise, start, try
     Verbs + to + infinitive: afford, like, want, hate
4   a I enjoy watching films at home.
     b I love going out with my friends.
     c I often practise speaking English in my English
        class.
     d I hate working at the weekend.
     e I can afford to buy one CD every month, but I can't
        afford to buy many.
     f My best friend wants to be a doctor.
     g My parents keep telling me to find a job.
     h I always try to help other people.
     i I have decided to go home as soon as I can.
5   a to see b trying c to learn d to go
     e to take/taking f to go g wearing h to be
     i practising j doing k to copy/copying
6   a dancing b to revise c to help d writing
     e going f talking g talking/to talk
     h to go/going
7   *Suggested answers*
     a Don't forget to help with the cooking!
     b Did you finish writing the report?
     c Please stop talking on your mobile.
     d Don't forget to revise your grammar.
     e I hate (watching) horror movies.

Unit 29

1   The sentences with mistakes are:
     c (more correct is 'She gave it to me')
     e (more correct is 'She gave me a present' or 'She gave
        a present to me')
     g (more correct is 'She gave my mother a present' or
        'She gave a present to my mother')
2   a She wrote me a letter.
     b I bought it for him.
     c He played his song for a girlfriend.
     d My mother gave me a radio for my birthday.
     e It cost them a lot of money.
     f He offered them a good price.
     g I owe a lot of money to my father.

3   a lent b bought c showed d wrote e owe
     f sent g read h left i Pay j teach k give
4   a lend b borrow
5   a a new CD
     b twice
     c Michelle
     d Chris's
     e Chris
     f Michelle
     g after a week
     h the CD
     i Michelle

j   Karen
Direct objects: underlined
Indirect objects: bold

Katie bought a new CD. She listened to it twice and then Michelle borrowed it. Michelle was showing it to Chris and she left it at his house. The next day, Chris asked Michelle if he could borrow it, because he liked it. After a week Katie asked Michelle to give the CD back to her. Michelle said, "I'm sorry, Katie, but I lent it to Chris." So Katie phoned Chris. "Yes, I borrowed it from Michelle, " said Chris, "but then I bought the CD at the music shop." "So, who has my CD?" said Katie. "I gave it back to Michelle and then she lent it to Karen."

Unit 30

1   a   Frank told her to enter the competition.
   b   Martin begged her not to enter the competition.
   c   Paul wanted/wants her to enter the competition.
   d   Sam invited her to enter the competition.
   e   Her father ordered her to enter the competition.
   f   Sue reminded her to enter the competition.
   g   Brad warned her not to enter the competition.
   h   Anita asked her to enter the competition.
2   a   play
   b   not to fall
   c   not to stay
   d   to come
   e   to cook
   f   not to wait
   g   to go
3   a   Mary reminded Jake to take his books.
   b   Ron and Jody invited Kevin to (come to) dinner.
   c   Susie told Michelle and Claire to go home.
   d   Chris invited Mike to watch TV.
   e   David told Janie to put it down.
   f   Emma warned Richie and Charles not to go in there.
   g   Ellie wanted to have some cake.
   h   Alice begged Marty to help her.
4   a   She ordered the child to go to bed at once.
   b   She suggested (that) she (should) wear the blue one.
   c   The customer asked for his / her money back.
   d   The driver begged the traffic warden not to give her / him a parking ticket.
   e   The boy promised the girl (that) he would never, ever leave her.
   f   The nurse reassured the patient (that) he / she would be fine.
   g   She reminded her daughter (that) it was her Dad's birthday in two days' time.
5   a let b make c make d let e let f let g make

Unit 31

1   a 8   b 7   c 4 (were watching)   d 10   e 12
   f 3   g 2   h 11   i 9   j 5   k 1   l 6
2   a   does, live
   b   lives
   c   Have, been
   d   haven't

   e   going
   f   did, leave
   g   left
   h   arrived
   i   Can / Will, help
   j   'll
3   a has been   b is/has been
   c are developing/have developed   d thinks
   e will become   f believes
4   a buy b pay, owed   c sending   d lend, read
   e borrow f show g teach h leave
5   a   can, can, couldn't, couldn't
   b   can, can't, can't
   c   couldn't, couldn't
   d   can, can, can, can

Unit 32

1   a the largest b any c some d much e a few
   f more popular g best h heavier i higher
   j the most interesting k – l a m through n along
2   a past b future c present
   d present/past e present f past
   g future h present i past
3   a   past simple (passive)
   b   future continuous
   c   present continuous
   d   present perfect
   e   present continuous (passive)
   f   past simple
   g   future simple
   h   present simple
   i   past continuous
4   a 3 b 2 c 1 d 1 e 2 f 3 g 1 h 2 i 2